CONTROLLING KNOWLEDGE

CONTROLLING KNOWLEDGE

Freedom of Information and Privacy Protection in a Networked World

— **LORNA STEFANICK** —

AU PRESS

Copyright © 2011 Lorna Stefanick
Published by AU Press, Athabasca University
1200, 10011 – 109 Street, Edmonton, AB T5J 3S6

ISBN 978-1-926836-26-3 (print)
ISBN 978-1-926836-27-0 (PDF)
ISBN 978-1-926836-61-4 (epub)

Library and Archives Canada Cataloguing in Publication

Stefanick, Lorna, 1961–
Controlling knowledge : freedom of information and privacy
protection in a networked world / by Lorna Stefanick.

Includes bibliographical references.
Issued also in electronic format.
ISBN 978-1-926836-26-3

1. Freedom of information.
2. Privacy, Right of.
I. Title.

K3255.S74 2011   342.08'53   C2011-904732-2

Cover and interior design by Natalie Olsen, Kisscut Design.
Printed and bound in Canada by Marquis Book Printers.

We acknowledge the financial support of the Government of Canada
through the Canada Book Fund (CBF) for our publishing activities.

 Canada Council **Conseil des Arts**
for the Arts   du Canada

To my father, George,
who taught me the importance
of integrity and accountability

and

to my mother, Millie,
who taught me the importance
of respecting personal space

CONTENTS

PREFACE AND ACKNOWLEDGEMENTS

I was first introduced to issues of information access and privacy protection when I joined the University of Alberta's Faculty of Extension in 1999, where I served initially as chief editor and subsequently as associate director of the programs in the Government Studies unit. With fears of Y2K circulating like wildfire, the eve of the new millennium was a fitting time to discover what seemed to me then to be the obscure field of data management. A senior public servant in the Alberta government, Alec Campbell, asked the director of the Government Studies unit, Professor Edd LeSage, to develop a course on freedom of information and protection of privacy (FOIP) for administrators who were confronted with the FOIP legislation enacted several years earlier. And so began my involvement in the field.

Under the stewardship of Wayne MacDonald, the course rapidly expanded into Canada's only program dedicated to information rights. The popularity of this program underscores the demand for specialized education and training for lawyers, public servants, administrators, and others working in the field. The fact that the program is available online to students across the country demonstrates that it is possible to use some of the technologies discussed in this book to advance the public good. In 2003, Wayne and I negotiated the University of Alberta's acquisition of a popular annual access and privacy conference. This event is attended by access and privacy commissioners from across Canada, their staff, and others working in the field; it provides an important opportunity for professional development.

It would take a family member experiencing a serious accident to really pique my interest in the subject, however. Most of us remain complacent about what information we can access and, in turn, about who has access to information about us. But when one of my daughters and her best friend were run over by a car and seriously injured, public officials told me that FOIP legislation prevented the release of information contained in an accident report and medical records. That was when my own complacency evaporated. Most of us don't recognize the importance of being able to get information until we need it. Similarly, most of us don't recognize the importance of protecting our personal information until such a time that the information is "out there" and we are unable to get it back. This book was written for those who are thinking that perhaps they ought to become less complacent.

Like all academic endeavours, this manuscript was long in the making and has left me deeply in debt. Athabasca University provided financial support for this project through a Research Incentive Grant and also presented me with a

President's Award for Academic Excellence, which gave me the time I needed to complete the manuscript. I am grateful for the unflagging support of those at AU Press: Pamela MacFarland Holway, Meenal Shrivastava, Manijeh Mannani, Karen Wall, and Alvin Finkel. The decision to publish a manuscript on freedom of information with North America's first open access academic press was a "no brainer." A special debt is owed to Mary Marshall, who provided the groundwork for the chapter on privacy. In addition, Mary encouraged me to pursue the topic, read drafts, and commiserated with my complaints about struggling to maintain a balance between work and home life. Fannie Dimitriadis stimulated my thinking on surveillance, and Ben Good challenged me to develop my ideas. Paul Thomas, Wayne MacDonald, Kiran Choudhry, and Brenda Markle offered useful comments on various chapters. Thanks also to the AU breakfast group that provides such interesting conversation every Friday — and whose members came up with a working title for this volume within twenty minutes of being requested to do so.

Finally, thanks to my family. Lynsey and Elena: I appreciate your patience with a mother who always demands to know why a clerk needs to have her personal information. I am also grateful that, as a pair of undergraduate students, you agreed to "test drive" a chapter of this book. And to Jim, as always, my toughest critic of how well arguments hang together, both in the public and the personal sphere: there is a special place in FOIP heaven for a person who reads multiple drafts of a manuscript on access and privacy.

CH_1
*An Introduction to Freedom of
Information and Privacy Protection*

ACCESSING AND PROTECTING ELECTRONIC DATA

For anyone under the age of twenty-five living in an industrialized country, typing term papers on a typewriter or looking up books by flipping through paper index cards in a filing cabinet in the library is a completely foreign concept. Similarly, life without a laptop computer, the Internet, a cellphone, or an iPod is incomprehensible. But despite the depth of their penetration into our daily lives, the ubiquity of these communication devices is a very recent phenomenon. The proliferation of the Internet and other technological innovations in the 1990s has had a seismic impact on our ability to create, store, and share information. The subsequent development of social networking, along with the digitization of commerce and government in the following decade, has had an equally profound impact on the ways in which people communicate and go about their daily business. These changes are particularly stunning given the speed with which they happened. The first digital computer was built in 1939, and in the 1960s information systems were developed to store data. These systems evolved with the introduction of personal computers in the 1980s. It was the development and proliferation of the Internet in the 1990s, however, that saw not only the collection and storage of increasing amounts of data but also the ability of citizens and consumers to access these data with the click of a mouse. A decade later, the Internet ushered in "digital government"[1] and "e-commerce," whereby interactions between the citizen/consumer and the state/producer began to be mediated by electronic technologies. This was also the era when "digital relationships" came into being, that is, peer-to-peer relationships mediated by technology.

By the end of 2010, it was hard to imagine how society had ever functioned without digital communication. These dramatic changes resulted in a fundamental shift in the way individuals interact with organizations and with each other. We now rarely go into a government building to take care of such mundane chores as renewing pet licences or paying parking tickets. We gather information and purchase items online. Few of us can remember the last time we wrote a letter to a relative, if in fact we have ever done this in the past. We communicate with our friends by looking at their Facebook page and commenting on their walls, by sending email, or by instant messaging or texting. These online activities allow us to access information about other people and organizations and to "take care of business," be it personal or professional, in the solitude of our homes. But these online activities also allow others to gather information about us remotely. The central issue that this book addresses is where the line should be drawn between what information should be readily available to others upon request and what information should be restricted in order to protect personal privacy. The fundamental concern is how much control individuals should have over their personal information in light of competing demands for it from others within society. In examining this question, this book analyzes protection of privacy and freedom of information (also known as access to information)[2] — two issues that most people know something about but few people know much about, despite their relevance to our everyday lives.

This text explains why freedom of information and protection of privacy (FOIP) is important. It elucidates how FOIP underpins the good governance that is so critical to a free, democratic, and economically competitive society. It illustrates the relationship between privacy and personal autonomy, which allows individuals to pursue their self-interest free from external control. It also reveals the relationship between access to information and accountability, which is necessary for good governance in the public, private, and non-profit sectors. In some respects, the debate over the proper balance between access and privacy mirrors the age-old debate over the optimum balance between the rights of the individual and those of the public interest (the latter broadly defined as the interest of the larger community in which the individual lives). This is a question that has engaged political scientists, economists, and others in a wide range of discussions that focus on such things as the role of the state in providing universal social programs, the optimal rate and type of taxation, and constitutional arrangements that seek to accommodate the needs of particular linguistic or ethnic groups. Typically, we tend to think of proponents of particular positions as sitting on opposite sides of the left-right political spectrum. This neat division between left and right, however, does not work nearly so well in conceptualizing the complex relationship between access and privacy.

As the following pages illustrate, the right to keep information private can be claimed by both an individual and a group of individuals. The same can be said for the right to access to information. As such, the public interest is not definitively linked to either the promotion of access to information or the protection of privacy. What is clear is that the stunning speed of technological innovation with respect to the collection, storage, and dissemination of information will necessitate very careful consideration of how we manage information. The decision to withhold or release particular information will have a significant impact on the individuals and organizations to whom this information pertains and raises major issues around who should make the decision and on what basis. We ignore these issues at our peril; history has taught us that freedom and democratic institutions are often most appreciated only after they are either threatened or lost.

This book provides an overview of the principles that underpin, issues that arise from, historical development of, and application of protection of privacy and freedom of information (FOI) legislation. While it does tilt toward the Canadian case, the general principles and issues presented are common to countries around the world that are grappling with providing an access and privacy regime for their citizens. While other studies might give a comprehensive analysis of either FOI or the protection of privacy, the most useful understanding comes from considering them together. In an increasingly global and digitized world, the choices we make with respect to how we manage information will become key factors in defining the communities in which we live.

ACCOUNTABILITY AND AUTONOMY

Freedom of information is critical for ensuring democratic accountability, and in particular due process and citizen participation. Privacy, on the other hand, is central to a person's sense of personal space and security. It is here that things become complex. Accessing information is more than just a means to allow citizens to keep tabs on their government. It is also a way for citizens to gain information about themselves and their neighbours. FOI speaks to both the ability of the individual to obtain information about the group and the right of the group to information about the individual.

FOI legislation can also be used to access government-held information about businesses and corporations. Citizens can see to whom government is awarding contracts and how it is spending taxpayers' dollars. It also allows businesses to obtain information about their competitors. In contrast, privacy protection legislation prohibits the release of particular information if it is deemed to infringe unnecessarily on privacy. It also allows both citizens and consumers to determine what personal information governments and businesses have on file that relates to them. Some privacy legislation also applies to non-profit organizations that engage in commercial activities. While these provisions represent a form of access, they also relate to privacy in that individuals have a right to know what personal information is held by others. Decisions about what information should be released hinge on the proper balance between the rights of the individual and the rights of groups. On this point reasonable people may differ. Moreover, the ability of various individuals to articulate their point of view effectively differs depending on their status within society.

Individual rights refer to the personal autonomy of an individual — specifically, the freedom of the individual to pursue his or her self-interest without interference. They also refer to the right of the individual to be protected from others whose pursuit of their self-interest might interfere with the individual's right to be left alone. In contrast, group rights refer to morals or values decided by the community. The preservation of these values may in fact limit the ability of individuals to pursue their own interest or may interfere with their desire to be left alone. The crucial question then becomes: At what point do the interests of the group justify the limitation of individual autonomy?

Here is an example that illustrates the debate over how privacy should be balanced with access to information. A car hits a pedestrian at a corner that the community considers to be very dangerous because the crosswalk is poorly lit and obscured by a bend in the road. The investigating officer writes a report that contains (among other things) the names, addresses, phone numbers, and ages of the couple in the car and the person who was walking across the street. As it turns out, the two people in the car are married, but not to each other; they are having an affair. The person walking across the street is a recovering alcoholic who has just left a local tavern. The community league wants to read the report to determine whether the accident was due to driver/pedestrian error or the poor design of the corner. If it is the latter, the community league plans to lobby the city for improvements. The critical question is: Do the rights of the community league to ask for information pertaining to the safety of an intersection in its neighbourhood take precedence over the rights of individuals to conduct their personal business without coming under the scrutiny of their neighbours?

How this question is answered depends on how any particular society balances the interests of the group against those of the individual. As such, the answer might be different in various societies. If it is determined that some, but not all, information should be released, who makes this determination? On what principles is this decision made and what weighting is put on the balance between competing principles? How transparent should societal and governing arrangements be? While there might not be one "correct" answer, Amitai Etzioni argues:

> Good societies carefully balance individual rights and social responsibilities, autonomy and the common good, privacy concerns for public safety and public health, rather than allow one value or principle to dominate. Once we accept the concept of balance, the question arises as to how we are to determine whether our polity is off balance and in what direction it needs to move, and to what extent, to restore balance.[3]

The theme of balance is one that permeates this book. The notion of balance is central to understanding the relationship between access and privacy, and it is a concept that typically is missing when these two goals are examined independently of one another.

UNPACKING THE CONCEPTS

The effective crafting of legislation to protect privacy or to ensure access to information requires developing a conceptual framework that defines and delimits the concepts. The following section introduces two key concepts that underpin legislation used worldwide: transparency and privacy. This discussion highlights some basic features of each concept and their evolution and explains why advocates argue that they are critical to a free and democratic society. These are complicated concepts and are explored in detail in chapters 2 and 3.

Access to information legislation is based on the concept of transparency. Through scrutiny of behaviour and performance, people are held accountable for their actions. Transparency also allows visibility for the curious, however, or visibility for reasons other than ensuring accountability. It thus becomes an important counterpoint to privacy. What quickly becomes apparent is that transparency is a complex concept that impinges on multiple aspects of society, in different directions and at different levels. The concept is also applicable to a variety of sectors. This is in contrast to access to information legislation, which for the most part is limited to the public sector.

David Heald provides a typology for understanding the different directions in which transparency can flow: upwards, downwards, inwards, and outwards. Transparency "upwards" refers to the flow of information from subordinates to persons in positions of authority.[4] This form of transparency is particularly important to the workplace, where supervisors monitor the work habits of those reporting to them. It is far more controversial when it involves public authorities monitoring the behaviour of citizens. Transparency "downwards" allows those who are ruled to review and assess the results produced by their leaders. Such transparency is the basis of a democratic system, in which, through elections, the rulers rule by virtue of the consent of the ruled. It also applies in the workplace, however. For example, a department head may hold a meeting to present financial statements and explain the coming year's strategic plan to workers. While the department head is not held accountable to the same degree as a politician, the central point is that both citizens and workers follow their leaders to the extent that they have confidence in them.

Transparency outward is the ability to see beyond the borders of one's organization. This is desirable because it allows people to view and evaluate the behaviour of their peers or competitors. Indeed, some of the heaviest users of access to information legislation are private sector companies seeking information regarding the awarding of government contracts. Transparency inward is the ability to see the inner workings of an organization. This is important with respect to such critical human resources management functions as the hiring and retention of staff: it fosters clear and equitable processes as opposed to those characterized by favoritism and nepotism. In a social context, however, transparency inward can have negative connotations: it refers to a society "policing itself" by monitoring the behaviour of citizens. In a relatively benign formulation, citizens might participate in a "neighbourhood watch" program, wherein citizens phone the police to report suspicious or possibly criminal behaviour. In a totalitarian society, however, citizens are expected to report their family members, friends, and neighbours to state authorities for actions that are considered to be counter to the interests of the state. Clearly, all societies need security from violent crime, but the concern with transparency inward often strays into the debate about what constitutes crime. That is, highly transparent societies (as opposed to transparent governments) suggest social control that severely limits freedom of thought and self-expression. With both horizontal and vertical transparency, complete asymmetry (either completely transparent or completely private) is not a desirable state of affairs. As Etzioni argued earlier, balance is a critical foundation of a "good" society.

Generally speaking, the lower the level of transparency within organizations and societies, the more beneficial it is to increase transparency. As transparency increases, privacy decreases and vice versa. Like the law of supply and demand, at a certain point the cost to other values such as personal privacy and autonomy may be more than a particular individual, organization, or society is prepared to bear. It is important that the different directions of transparency are understood and, given the different trade-offs, that the appropriate mix is chosen. We know that sunlight is an important source of vitamin D, but too much of it can give us sunburn or, even worse, skin cancer. As Heald notes: "When sunlight becomes searchlight it becomes uncomfortable, and when it becomes torch it may be destructive."[5] The same can be said about privacy — a certain degree of privacy is necessary to ensure individual security and autonomy. Too much privacy, however, can act as a shield protecting those who seek to hide questionable activities from public scrutiny.

Like transparency, privacy is a multi-dimensional concept. According to Privacy International, it comprises four separate but related components: bodily, communications, territorial, and informational.[6] Bodily privacy focuses on the protection of people's physical selves against such invasive procedures as cavity searches, drug testing, and genetic tests. As demonstrated in chapters 4 and 5, genetic and drug testing raise informational and communication privacy concerns. Privacy of communications covers the privacy and security of email, telephone, mail, and other forms of communication. Google and Facebook faced a storm of criticism in 2010 for their privacy practices; these issues are taken up in chapters 5 and 6. Territorial privacy concerns the establishment of limits on intrusion into a variety of physical spaces, such as the domestic space, the workplace, and public space. This type of privacy protection would concern itself with searches of personal space or property, video surveillance, and ID checks. The issue of surveillance is a contentious topic and is the focus of chapter 6. Information privacy refers to the collection and handling of personal data contained in such things as government records, medical records, and credit card information. The rules governing this type of privacy are known as "data protection." The rate at which such data is collected has been accelerating, and the quantity of data now collected is staggering. The case of medical information illustrates some of the benefits and risks associated with this form of data collection: this is the focus of chapter 4. The four dimensions of privacy will be covered in more detail in the next chapter; however, it is information privacy and data protection that are the main focuses of this book.

Countries that provide constitutional protection of privacy regard it as a fundamental human right that is necessary to safeguard the individual's autonomy and dignity. With the exception of the right not to be tortured, however, no human right is absolute. Like other human rights, privacy must be balanced with other rights. In contrast, neither transparency nor its other manifestations, freedom of information or access to information, is a human right. The ability to access information is typically governed by laws that are passed in legislatures, as opposed to being enshrined in constitutions. As such, an understanding of FOI begins with a look at the evolution of the concept of transparency and its relationship to general principles of public administration. As with privacy rights that are not constitutionally entrenched, transparency and FOI must be considered in the context of competing societal interests.

The complex and intertwined relationship between transparency and privacy is illustrated by the fact that in many jurisdictions the measures taken to ensure both access to information and privacy protection are contained in one piece of legislation and the oversight body that ensures compliance with the legislation comprises one office, not two. It is thus remarkable that privacy and transparency (and their legislative manifestations, privacy protection and access to information) are typically considered in isolation from one another. The following discussion of the benefits and risks of increasing both transparency and privacy illustrates the difficulty with analyzing one concept without reference to the other.

TRANSPARENCY, PRIVACY, AND GOOD GOVERNANCE

FOI is recognized as a critical component of good governance. It rests upon three pillars that are well known in public administration: fixed rules, transparency, and accountability. Some or all of these are found in the earliest treatises of political thought, including those of the Chinese and the Greeks. Later, they can be found in German institutions, as well as in the writings of Adam Smith, Jean-Jacques Rousseau, Immanuel Kant, and Jeremy Bentham. They can also be seen in early reformed church thinking and the local government "town hall" meeting traditions of New England.[7] We can find modern strains of transparency influencing architecture: witness the "open cubicle" office concept, wherein employees can be watched easily by their peers and managers.

More recently, feminists argue that transparency can be used to expose gendered structures of authority as well as the patriarchal thinking that underpins them. Catherine MacKinnon asserts that transparency is key to revealing the patriarchy of the private space of family relations. The public sphere was traditionally deemed to be the domain of men, while women and children were confined to the private sphere. So-called "women's issues" pertained to family matters and thus were part of the private sphere. The old adage "a man's home is his castle" reflects the male role as "head of the family." Women were not only confined to the private sphere, they were subject to domination by their husbands, fathers, and brothers; what happened behind closed doors was not a subject for public discourse. The 1960s feminist cry that "the personal is the political" was an attempt to expose the oppression of women in their most intimate relationships by linking it to their invisibility (or secondary status) within the public sphere. It also sought to break the silence that surrounded rape and spousal and child abuse by challenging the tolerance of oppression and violence that exist in the private sphere. According to MacKinnon the "right of privacy is a right of men 'to be let alone' to oppress women one at a time."[8] While in Western nations the gendered boundaries between public and private space have blurred, in many parts of the world (including immigrant communities within Western nations) this division is still clearly demarcated.

By exposing truths, advocates claim, transparency will hold people to account for their behaviour. Transparency at times takes on the aura of a motherhood issue: when talking about good governance, who would promote secrecy over transparency and accountability? Secrecy conjures up notions of the freedom to commit wrongs with no fear of being held accountable. Secrecy is linked to censorship, which flies in the face of a great democratic value, freedom of expression. The old adage "knowledge is power" speaks to the importance of having relevant information in order to influence what happens in the political, social, and economic realms. Those who "know" have the potential to act based on an understanding of what the different options are. Knowledge is key to the exercise of power, the structuring of competition among groups for a particular policy outcome, and the organization of political communities. A modern variation of this formulation might be "those who control knowledge have power." As such, would anyone committed to equity, freedom, and democracy argue against the dissemination of information, and by extension, the dissemination of the knowledge that underpins power?

The dissemination of information to the masses means that authoritarian governments lose their monopoly on information and with it their ability to control and stifle dissent. Armed with knowledge, citizens are in a better position to assess not only their government's actions and policies but also those of other governments. Information access provides the poor and their advocates with leverage to effect social change. In addition to fostering a culture of openness, the free dissemination of information allows consumers to make more informed choices and citizens to participate more fully in democracy. Access legislation is also critical to the fight against corruption. For example, FOI laws are a prerequisite for developing countries that receive financial aid from the West. Laws that make it possible to trace financial transactions reveal who is receiving the aid and how much is being received. In this way, access regimes force both governments and corporations to become more accountable for their actions.

The Internet and cellphones are coming to be more important to non-governmental organizations than traditional media, such as newspapers and television, in disseminating the information that helps to redistribute power. Traditional media have often been criticized for presenting what purports to be objective news coverage through various filters, thereby introducing an element of bias. News and opinions are vetted by editors who are constrained by circulation numbers or advertising dollars. In contrast, on the Internet, news and information can be passed along without such constraints, whether on blogs or on Twitter or simply by email. While such information must still be read critically, the relatively unrestricted nature of new media helps to ensure that the information needed to hold organizations to account circulates freely.

Democratic countries worldwide are embracing requirements that promote transparency: witness the rise of information access regimes and the adoption of new standards of conduct. Ann Florini describes this trend: "The world is embracing new standards of conduct, enforced not by surveillance and coercion but by willful disclosure: regulation by revelation."[9] The motivation for a company to willingly disclose corporate information derives in part from its desire to be seen as "progressive" and "a good corporate citizen." The development of industry standards of conduct makes good strategic sense, however. An industry that adheres to voluntary standards of conduct is less likely to feel the heavy hand of state regulators, or at the very least, will be able to influence the types of regulations that are introduced.

Transparency, of course, is of no use if no one is watching. As such, transparency becomes linked to surveillance. Most of us have no problem with the notion of citizens watching their government, or stockholders watching their fund managers, but what of managers watching employees — say, by monitoring their email? Or governments that watch their citizens through video cameras and surveillance data? Or school officials who monitor their students by following social networking sites like Facebook? When does transparency slip from being a public good to becoming the public "bad" associated with surveillance that infringes on personal privacy? In the digital age, free-flowing information enables the creation of massive databases. The information in such databases can be mixed and matched with that in other data banks to create a very detailed personal dossier of the citizen-consumer that can be used for various purposes. The notion of free-flowing information as a public good can very quickly morph into images of the all-knowing, all-seeing "Big Brother" observing, recording, and acting on our every step (and misstep).

The same juxtaposition is true for privacy. Privacy advocates assert that every individual requires the ability to retreat into a personal space where one has the freedom to do what one wants without being scrutinized by others. Society is ultimately composed of individuals; these individuals require some degree of autonomy. But when does the protection of individual privacy represent a public "bad" in that it harms others in society? Where is the line drawn that delineates the private from the public? Are there some activities within the private space that are so repugnant to society that privacy can be overridden?

The flip side of this rosy picture of free-flowing information becomes much gloomier when these questions are considered. Pessimists point out that the new speed with which information can be distributed will be harnessed to spread rumours, lies, and hate. Information that is true but that an individual would prefer to keep private can also be distributed to millions in the blink of an eye. Just a decade ago, gossip or an embarrassing picture or secret did not usually travel beyond one's immediate peer group. Now these can go global in a matter of seconds. Once the information is "out there" on the Internet, it is difficult if not impossible to rein it back in. For an individual who has been "outed," personal privacy is gone — that aspect of the individual's personality will never again reside in the private sphere to be revealed only at the will of the individual. Prejudice and hatred that is broadly disseminated without repercussions or comment can appear to justify and legitimize the victimization of particular people or groups. Hurtful jokes and hateful opinions can be easily forwarded. Oft-debated questions are: What are the limits of freedom of expression? What is the role of public institutions in placing limits on those whose opinions limit the autonomy and security of others?[10] What rights do citizens have to protect their privacy vis-à-vis the intrusive gaze of the state, corporations, and fellow citizens? As the stakes increase with the volume and ease of information flow, these questions take on more urgency.

If knowledge is power, the diffusion of knowledge will make those who obtain it more powerful. This could empower previously weak groups or individuals. It is equally plausible, however, that those who get it could already be powerful and additional knowledge will only make them more powerful. As Kristin Lord points out, "diffusion of information is not politically neutral, since when information changes hands, so too does influence."[11] The so-called "digital divide" refers to the gap between those in society who have access to the Internet (broadband, in their homes) and those who have either poor access (dial-up connection at a public library) or no access at all. The latter tend to be less-educated, poorer, and/or older adults. This group is also the demographic that is the least able to take measures to protect their personal privacy. The digital divide not only raises questions regarding the balance of power between societal interests, it also raises the spectre that those who reside in the technologically rich North will continue to amass power and influence vis-à-vis the technologically poor South. One only has to compare the extent of Internet penetration in countries such as Norway (almost 95 percent as of June 2010) and Ethiopia (only 0.5 percent) to see why there is cause for concern.[12] These rates paint a conservative picture of the digital divide, as they refer to access only; they do not make a distinction between those whose Internet access is through a cumbersome dial-up connection versus those with a broadband connection whereby downloading large digital files is done with ease. Add to this the problem of literacy rates: a person who cannot read and, in particular, read English, will not benefit much from Internet access, even if it is available. The current imbalance in power between the developed and the developing countries (as well as the rich and the poor within them) has the potential to grow to disastrous proportions with the rise of new technologies.

What is potentially more disturbing is the possibility for centralized control over the Internet. In this scenario, the information may be "out there" but we may not be able to access it. Even more troubling is that we may not realize that we are being prevented from accessing particular types of information. We are already seeing disparate attempts to censor what content can be viewed by particular viewers: parents can now control what sites their children can access, public libraries block pornographic sites, and schools restrict the use of social networking sites. The further away the censorship decisions are made from users the more controversial they become. Much has been said about the role of states such as China in restricting its citizens' access to particular websites. Control over the Internet, however, is a contentious issue for democracies as well. In response to the strain placed on servers by the increasing number of large file downloads, illegal file sharing, and piracy, Internet service providers have floated the idea of a tiered service model. They propose to maintain different levels of service for different websites. Websites of companies willing to pay for enhanced service would be given priority, resulting in decreased file transfer and download times for select sites. Service providers argue that they should be able to charge a fee to companies that provide content that uses substantial amounts of Internet bandwidth over the provider's network. Proponents of "net neutrality" argue that letting service providers charge differential rates for web pages based on content is akin to a phone company charging different phone rates based on whom a person calls or what is said while one is using the phone. The net neutrality movement seeks to ensure that all of the World Wide Web remains equally accessible to all who have an Internet connection.[13]

Leaving aside Internet access issues, another impediment to increased transparency resulting in better governance is the sheer volume of information and the ability of humans to effectively process it. The first issue is the filters that organizations use to organize information. We expect that organizations will do this, as otherwise we would be overwhelmed by information. Clearly, how information is filtered and presented will affect our understanding of the world around us. In years gone by, information was organized, ranked in importance, and released to the public by individuals within an organization. Thus, a system whereby information is located on a website that anyone with Internet access can obtain is arguably a good thing with respect to increasing transparency. The information "middle man" appears to be cut out. Filters still exist, however, particularly with respect to how information is organized on a website.

Huge volumes of information do not accomplish much if the required information is "buried" and difficult to find. The ease with which information can be found is critical for an organization that truly embraces transparency or one that wishes to provide customer service via the web. Search engines depend on effective page ranking to facilitate finding information, a function that the internal search engines of a website often lack. Each web page must contain particular tags or "clues" that the search engine picks up as it sorts through a plethora of pages. Anyone who has used the internal search engine of a poorly organized website knows that it may be much faster to find information by entering the search terms in a global search engine such as Google. Alternatively, the fastest way to obtain customer service or to find information may be to make a physical trip to the organization's office and make the request in person.

Ironically, the volume of information provided by large organizations with respect to any particular issue has been cited as a major problem not only with transparency itself but also with privacy protection. An organization that prefers a particular course of action that it knows will not be popular with users of its services or products might strategically overwhelm its users with such a volume of information that making an informed choice is very difficult. This phenomenon is illustrated in the case of the social networking company Facebook, which has embraced transparency (i.e., the sharing of user information) with such enthusiasm that users who are concerned with privacy are left with the choice of either leaving the site or wading through a large labyrinth of privacy settings in order to exercise "choice."

Compounding the problem of massive amounts of competing information is the problem of evaluation. Humans use shortcuts to help them organize and process information. We create frameworks by which we organize the voluminous data coming at us; these frameworks are critical in assisting us in forming opinions on particular subjects. If we come across information that does not mesh with our pre-existing views, we may resist it, even if it is from a reliable source. Although we may have organizations that are models of transparency, we cannot be sure that the information that we take in and think about when forming our opinions is unbiased. In this sense, then, the "gatekeeper" function may increasingly come to be performed by those in society who have the most funds available to promote their perspective on an issue through advertising and the spreading of information from a particular point of view.

This discussion reveals the two sides of transparency — on one side the optimists point to the great benefits of increasing information flow, while on the other the pessimists point to its ominous ill effects. Optimists argue that transparency is critical to good governance in both the public and the private sectors. Similarly, privacy is critical to personal autonomy, but too much privacy can enable deviant behaviour. So does the preceding suggest that we should throw up our hands and give up? Not at all, unless we are satisfied with a situation wherein citizen-consumers are blissful in their ignorance, leaving governments, corporations, and other large organizations to do what they want with no fear of criticism, no concern for accountability, and no need to respect the privacy of the individuals with whom they interact. It does raise a flag of caution, however, that transparency is not a panacea with regard to accountability, and accountability can be justifiably curtailed by privacy concerns. Transparency and privacy can take many forms; with respect to governance, sometimes the cure can be worse than the ailment. To draw an analogy, before one begins major renovations to replace a wall with windows, one ought to consider whether the benefit of a feature wall that shows off priceless paintings is worth the risk of having them fade from exposure to the sun. More importantly, before demolition begins one should consider if removing a wall is going to affect the structural integrity of the building.

OVERVIEW OF THE BOOK

There is a general acknowledgement that access and privacy legislation is important, if for no other reason than that it is increasingly common and very annoying to be told that an organization cannot do something requested of it because of FOIP legislation. Despite its alleged salience to organizational integrity and democracy, however, the academic literature on the subject is surprisingly sparse. There have been no systematic comparisons yet of access and privacy legislative regimes nationally or internationally. Explanations of issues in language that are easily digestible by non-experts are limited and typically take the form of reports produced by access and privacy commissioners. The work that has been done focuses on either access or privacy; rarely are the two considered in tandem. This is unfortunate, as the two are linked not only operationally but also conceptually.

Freedom of information and protection of privacy are best understood when considered together because they each represent a pole on a common continuum. Promotion of one comes at the expense of the other. There are no right or wrong positions on this continuum — other than that a democracy will want to be somewhere in the middle and that the designated position should represent the values and priorities of its citizens.

While the purposes and requirements of private and not-for-profit sector organizations are different from those in the public sector, they too must be cognizant of the necessary balance between access and privacy. Even though access to information legislation applies only to organizations in the public sector, the pressure on those in other sectors to be transparent is not insignificant, as dissatisfied consumers/clients have the option of patronizing other organizations. This choice is not afforded as easily, vis-à-vis the public sector, to disgruntled citizens, who have very limited options if they are unhappy with the balance their governments strike through FOIP legislation.

In all sectors, technological change has dramatically altered the ability to collect, retain, and distribute information. This in turn necessitates equally dramatic overhauls of information management systems. Related legislation and policies will provide the basis for "good governance" and must foster:

- individual dignity, as expressed through the ability to control certain aspects of one's persona (privacy), and

- accountability of the governors to their stakeholders for promoting the public good, as expressed through transparency.

The balance struck between these two components, which are often in competition with one another, must reflect the values and priorities of both the organization and those it serves.

The purpose of this book is to untangle the complex relationship between protection of privacy and access to information. The following chapter provides an overview of the many dimensions of personal privacy. It begins by considering the various types of privacy interests and why society values the protection of privacy. While the emphasis of the chapter is on informational privacy in both the public and private sectors, the broader context of shifting norms of privacy is considered. The third chapter focuses on freedom of information, with a particular focus on data management in the public sector. It analyzes the concept of access within the context of communication, bureaucratic administration, global interactions between states, and democratic governance. While transparency and improved communication at first blush may appear to be values that all right-thinking people should support, there is a dark side that must be considered. The next three chapters apply the concepts presented in the first two chapters to real-life situations. The case studies of electronic health records, surveillance, and social networking explore how society attempts to balance protection of privacy with other societal benefits such as accountability, efficiency, security, and social and political engagement. The common thread that ties these case studies together is the question: Is the societal benefit gained worth the sacrifice of privacy?

It should be noted at the outset that this is not a "how-to" book for policy makers. This book is aimed at both citizens and consumers generally and, more specifically, to students in a range of professional disciplines who will grapple with access and privacy issues at some point in their careers: journalists, librarians, public servants, human resources personnel, lawyers and those who work with the criminal justice system, social workers, and information technology and health care professionals, to name just a few. Others, such as historians doing archival work and environmentalists seeking information about the ecological impacts of development proposals, may also find this text of interest. Its purpose is to outline the general principles associated with access and privacy and related issues. The principles at times compete, and the issues around implementation are often very similar worldwide. While students might anticipate benefiting from the ability to use their understanding of access and privacy concepts in the conduct of their professional lives, they may find that the greatest benefit will be gleaned from their ability to act as savvy consumers and enlightened voters.

While FOI and protection of privacy are discussed in general terms, the central theme of this book is the balance of the two as they relate to governance. It challenges citizens to think about their underlying assumptions concerning such concepts as privacy, security, accountability, and democracy. It asks them to consider competing perspectives and that the privileging of privacy over access and vice versa speaks to underlying values that may or may not be shared. Moreover, the perspective that legislative regimes reflect may have less to do with the building of a just and good society than with the power relations within society. The reflective decision maker will understand these power dynamics and will "unpack" assumptions and the ideological baggage that goes with them in order to settle on the best course of action. A decision maker who does this goes considerable distance toward avoiding unintended and possibly undesirable consequences. In order to be shrewd consumers and fully participating citizens, individuals need to understand the relationship between access and privacy in order to keep those in control of information accountable. Professionals who deal with access and privacy legislation can use this knowledge to assist them in exercising their own power prudently with respect to the information they control. Ultimately, though, the ability to analyze the balance between access to information and protection of privacy through the lens of competing societal interests will help immeasurably in the development of a good and just society.

CH_2
Privacy Protection

THE MANY DIMENSIONS OF PRIVACY

The protection of privacy is fundamentally about autonomy, power, and knowledge. As noted in the introductory chapter, the old adage "knowledge is power" speaks volumes. The protection of personal privacy speaks to the ability of individuals to control what is known about themselves. Individuals who can control what others know about them have a degree of personal autonomy. Privacy protection also helps to define the relationship between the citizen and the state and between the consumer and the corporate interest. Fundamentally, it attempts to balance what is best for the individual with what is best for the larger community the individual lives within. The intriguing question is: Who decides where the balance lies?

Privacy is one those concepts that seems at first blush to be so easy to define, yet on closer examination becomes a moving target. At its most basic, privacy refers to the line that is drawn between the public and the private; it relates to the autonomy of the individual in relation to the larger community. But where this line should be drawn is both culturally specific and epoch-sensitive. A universal norm for what comprises socially appropriate behaviour does not exist, and thus the impetus to shield particular activities from the eyes of one's family, friends, and neighbours will differ from country to country and from era to era. For example, pre–twentieth-century English-speaking cultures were very reserved with respect to what individuals communicated to one another. It was expected that people would "keep a stiff upper lip" and that feelings and emotions would be suppressed. Fast forward to twenty-first-century English-speaking culture, wherein people go on television to confess to, or accuse one another of, all manner of outrageous transgressions. Pre–twentieth-century women in Western countries kept their legs concealed from public view under long dresses. A hundred years later there was far less societal pressure on women to conceal their body parts, and in this century many of them choose to draw a very small circle around what they consider "private."

This could be considered a triumph for women's personal autonomy, but individual control over the space considered private remains contestable and is still subject to cultural norms. Witness the 2010 International Football Association (FIFA)'s decision to ban the Iranian girls' soccer team from the Youth Olympics because the girls wear hijabs (head scarves). Three years earlier, soccer referees in Alberta, Ontario, and Quebec randomly banned girls wearing hijabs from playing because provincial rules deemed that anything worn on a player's head compromises safety, despite the fact that players wearing prescription eyeglasses were not prohibited from playing. The wearing of the hijab is an example of a culturally specific norm of privacy rooted in religion (concealing a part of the body for purposes of modesty) conflicting with rules devised by an organization that does not share that norm. Though FIFA refused to take a stand on the provincial disputes, it later deemed that wearing the hijab is an expression of religious affiliation that contravenes the rule that players' uniforms must be politically and religiously neutral. From a privacy perspective, however, it can be argued that forcing young girls to expose their heads in order to participate in a sporting event not only favours Western norms within the association, it also represents a profound violation of privacy and personal autonomy — that is, it does not allow the individual to decide how much of her body she will expose while playing soccer.

The debate over what is an appropriate athletic uniform for women is not confined to soccer, nor is it confined to particular parts of the world. In 1999, the FIVB (Fédération Internationale de Volleyball) declared bikinis to be the official uniform of women's beach volleyball competitions. The requirement to wear skimpy outfits resulted in the Indian team and others threatening to boycott international competitions. Musings from such soccer luminaries as FIFA president Sepp Blatter that woman soccer players should adopt a similar dress code in order to increase the popularity of the sport sparked harsh criticism from those who claim attitudes such as his demean women.[1] While Western feminists and Iranian mullahs are unlikely allies, they find themselves with similar complaints: specifically, that athletic dress codes for women detract from their athletic achievements by focusing on their sexuality. The uniforms of both the Iranian girls' soccer team and international women's beach volleyball teams illustrate that the decision as to where the public/private line is drawn with respect to modesty is determined not only by the individual but also by the community she lives in or, in this case, competes within. The privacy question remains the same, however: some things are put in full view of the community, other things are not. Who should decide what can or should be shielded from public view?

Notions of what appropriately rests in the private sphere and what should exist in the public sphere differ not only among cultures and generations but also among those who have different ideological outlooks. So, the free market proponent will claim that it is up to each individual to draw his or her own line and up to individuals to determine which activities they will either engage in or abstain from in order to stay on one side of the line or the other. Others argue that privacy is too fundamental to human dignity to leave to the marketplace. They seek government regulation to limit the intrusion of both governments and corporations into our personal space. Complicating the debate is the observation that the line demarcating the personal from the public space does not guarantee personal privacy. When the domestic sphere is shielded from public scrutiny, this can result in instances of domestic violence being ignored by public authorities who feel that what happens behind closed doors is not their business. As Anita Allen observes: "For some women, male hegemony and repressive confinement to the private sphere have stood as obstacles to genuine privacy and the exercise of privacy-related liberties."[2] Returning to our example of the hijab, it becomes clear that privacy as it relates to personal modesty is only one very small part of the privacy debate — privacy relates to a huge range of human activity. Moreover, new technologies have begun to erode individual privacy at an ever-accelerating rate, adding new urgency to the debate over where the line should be drawn between public and personal spaces.

At one time, privacy discussions remained the purview of a very limited academic set — lawyers mostly, with the odd contribution from political scientists, sociologists, and those with expertise in information communications technologies. Because privacy protection often involves highly complex technological developments, the debate can be very abstract and technical. But with the ever-increasing pressure on personal privacy that has resulted from new technologies, academics and professionals in an extraordinarily wide range of disciplines are adding their voices. Individuals who are becoming privacy-aware are also raising concerns in their capacity as consumers, as is demonstrated in chapter 6, which discusses social networking.

This is not to suggest, however, that concern for privacy is a recent phenomenon. Privacy concerns are found in studies of ancient Greece, Jewish societies, the Bible, and English Puritans in seventeenth-century New England. Legal discussions of the nature of the right to privacy began in the late nineteenth century with Samuel Warren and Louis Brandeis's "The Right to Privacy." In this oft-cited 1890 article, Warren and Brandeis define privacy as "the right to be let alone" and bemoan the decline of privacy with the advent of photography and sensationalist journalism. Combined with the printing press, photography allowed the circulation of candid images of people with or without their consent. Warren and Brandeis observed that these developments led to information that was previously private to be "shouted from the rooftops."[3] One wonders what Warren and Brandeis would have to say about the advent of digital photography that allows just about anyone to take multiple pictures anytime and distribute them to everyone. Uploading these images to the World Wide Web amplifies "shouting from the rooftops" to such an extent that it can be heard around the globe. These new developments notwithstanding, the reason that the Warren and Brandeis definition has held sway for more than a century is undoubtedly because of its simplicity and the difficulty others have had in trying to create a more sophisticated definition.

Building on the Warren and Brandeis definition, it is generally accepted that privacy is necessary to maintain human dignity, as it is fundamental to personal autonomy. It is our ability to retreat to a place of solitude and anonymity that allows us to grow and develop as individuals. Various freedoms such as freedom of expression underpin democratic societies, and these too rely on privacy. As the internationally distinguished constitutional scholar Zelman Cowen argued in 1969: "A man without privacy is a man without dignity; the fear that Big Brother is watching and listening threatens the freedom of the individual no less than the prison bars."[4]

Privacy is related to, but not the same as, confidentiality. Confidentiality refers to the legal duty of a person who is given personal information about another person by virtue of a professional relationship. The traditional approach to the disclosure and transfer of certain types of sensitive information such as that relating to health recognizes that personal information is special and must be managed accordingly because it has originated in confidence. At the core of the confidentiality interest is the recognition that it is not centrally linked to the autonomy and security of an individual, but rather is an interest only insofar as it is recognized and fostered by the law-making authority. As such, a law-making authority may abrogate this interest when the other interests are deemed to be more important than the confidentiality interest. In other words, confidentiality is considered to be a significant interest worthy of protection, but it is not a fundamental right as many claim privacy to be.

Privacy must also be distinguished from secrecy. Secrecy has negative connotations, suggesting that those who seek privacy are hiding something that they are ashamed of. Accordingly, transparency advocates seek to minimize the ability of governments to hide particular activities from public scrutiny. Secrecy provisions in legislation are usually based on the "need to preserve the secrecy of government operations in order for government to function effectively."[5] Maintaining a smooth-running government might mean concealing the bids of companies competing for government contracts from their competitors or might refer to concealing information that relates to national security.

The interests of the government and the citizen with respect to secrecy can be the same, but at times they might be quite different. As the Australian Law Reform Commission observes:

> The secrecy interests of agencies and the privacy interests of individuals will sometimes be complementary. For example, both an agency and the subject of information held by the agency might have an interest in

non-disclosure of that information to third parties. Those interests, however, may sometimes conflict. For example, a person may want access to his or her personal information to check that it has been recorded correctly and is not being disclosed without his or her consent; but to grant that access could intrude upon the secrecy interests of the agency.[6]

That said, there is concern that the decision to conceal might have less to do with important things such as national security and more to do with protecting wrongdoing in government. The same can be said about the motivation for secrecy within the private sector. This issue will be dealt with in more depth in the chapter that discusses transparency.

In this study, privacy will be defined as the right of individuals to be let alone to pursue their self-interest without observation or interference from others. Informational privacy is defined as the ability of individuals to have some measure of control over their own information in order to pursue their self-interest without observation or interference from those who are in possession of their personal data, unless there is an established and justifiable reason for such observation or interference. This very rudimentary attempt to provide a definition that has eluded so many others is not particularly sophisticated, but it does provide a conceptual framework within which issues associated with new and emerging technologies can be analyzed. It also provides a basis for understanding the relationship between transparency and privacy, and the legislative manifestations of these concepts: access to information and protection of privacy.

THE MARCH TOWARD REGULATION

While privacy has been recognized implicitly as an important component of free and democratic societies, it was recognized explicitly in major instruments of international law after World War II. United Nations declarations such as the Universal Declaration of Human Rights (1948) and the International Covenant on Civil and Political Rights (1966) regard privacy as a fundamental human right that is necessary to safeguard the individual's autonomy and dignity.[7] Nationally, privacy is recognized as a right in constitutions: most countries provide protections for communications and the inviolability of the home.[8] In those countries where privacy is not protected explicitly in constitutions, courts have found other provisions for protecting privacy.

In Canada, privacy is implicitly recognized in the Canadian Charter of Rights and Freedoms and by virtue of such court decisions such as *R. v. Dyment*. This 1988 case involved taking and testing a blood sample from a patient without his consent or knowledge and using the results to convict him of impaired driving. As Justice Gérard La Forest, of the Supreme Court of Canada, commented:

> Society has come to realize that privacy is at the heart of liberty in a modern state. . . . Grounded in man's physical and moral autonomy, privacy is essential for the well-being of the individual. For this reason alone it is worthy of constitutional protection, but it also has profound significance for the public order. The restraints imposed on government to pry into the lives of the citizen go to the essence of a democratic state.[9]

Justice LaForest goes on to quote from the 1972 report of Canada's Task Force on Privacy and Computers: "This notion of privacy derives from the assumption that all information about a person is in a fundamental way his own, for him to communicate or retain for himself as he sees fit." [10] This follows the writing of Alan Westin, who wrote the seminal book *Privacy and Freedom* in 1967. Westin defined privacy as the desire of individuals to choose freely how much of themselves to expose to others. It is thus important for individuals to control both what information is known about themselves and what is released. [11]

Most privacy protection comes by virtue of laws passed in legislatures that seek to give individuals control over their person. In the last few decades, countries around the world have developed information privacy legislation that seeks to protect the privacy of information held by governments. The roots of this legislation can be traced back to the introduction of voluntary guidelines developed by the Organisation for Economic Co-operation and Development (OECD) in 1980 in *Guidelines Governing the Protection of Privacy and Transborder Flows of Personal Data*. These guidelines anticipated the privacy challenges associated with new technologies that allowed the combining of data from a variety of sources to create comprehensive databases; they were designed to discourage member countries from introducing laws that conflicted with one another. [12] The guidelines recognize that "although national laws and policies may differ, Member countries have a common interest in protecting privacy and individual liberties, and in reconciling fundamental but competing values such as privacy and the free flow of information." [13] These voluntary guidelines were followed in 1995 by the European Union's *Directive on the Protection of Individuals with Regard to the Processing of Personal Data and on the Free Movement of Such Data*. This directive states:

1 In accordance with this Directive, Member States shall protect the fundamental rights and freedoms of natural persons, and in particular their right to privacy with respect to the processing of personal data.

2 Member States shall neither restrict nor prohibit the free flow of personal data between Member States for reasons connected with the protection afforded under paragraph 1.[14]

Member states were compelled to transpose this directive into law by 1998, which they did. Importantly, the directive stipulates that personal data from the European Union (EU) cannot be sent to any country that does not have privacy protection equivalent to that of EU members.

The 1995 directive has serious implications for trade between countries and created the impetus for the development of privacy laws within the European Union and elsewhere. The United States resisted the pressure to enact comprehensive privacy laws by entering into a "safe-harbour" agreement with EU in November 2000; this agreement comprises a set of principles developed by the US Department of Commerce and the EU. Companies that choose to comply are certified as such and are protected from having their data flow severed. Though the activities of transnational organizations are important for developing international norms and regulations, the decisions of trading blocs such as the EU may ultimately act as the domino that pushes countries elsewhere into following suit in order to maintain economic ties.

Other countries around the world began to follow in the EU's footsteps. In Asia, the *Privacy Framework* of APEC (Asian-Pacific Economic Cooperation, an organization devoted to fostering sustainable economic growth in the region) recognizes both privacy and the importance of freely flowing information and asserts its commitment to assisting in the development of uniform practices globally. It also supports the advancement of international mechanisms to enforce privacy while maintaining information flow, which includes enabling enforcement agencies to fulfill their mandate to protect information.[15] While this framework has been called "OECD Lite," Johanna Tan rightly notes that it "represents a consensus among countries that come forth from different legal systems, values, culture, and which are at different stages in enacting their privacy protection."[16] As such it constitutes a significant first step in its recognition of basic data protection principles.

In Canada, the Canadian Standards Association followed the EU lead by developing the Canadian Model Code, which outlines ten fair information principles: (1) accountability; (2) identifying purposes; (3) consent; (4) collection limitations; (5) use, disclosure, and retention limitations; (6) accuracy; (7) safeguards; (8) openness; (9) individual access; and (10) challenging compliance.[17] These principles simply state that organizations that collect information should be clear about why they are collecting the information, who will see it, and how long it will be held. Those whose information was collected must be able to see what is being held and how it is being held and be able to complain to someone within the organization if the information is inaccurate or is not being adequately protected. The principles formed the basis of subsequent legislation passed in Canada and elsewhere in the public, private, and non-profit sectors. The legislative regimes passed by Canada and Argentina were deemed to be "adequate" by the EU.

Eight years later the OECD passed another set of guidelines. *OECD Guidelines for the Security of Information Systems and Networks: Towards a Culture of Security* sets standards for the design and use of information communication technologies. These standards have been adopted for use by such international bodies as the United Nations, the Council of the European Union, Asia-Pacific Economic Cooperation, and Asia-Europe Meeting.

The guidelines and directives issued by national, regional, and international bodies address the concerns relating to the security of data collected from individuals and stored by both governments and businesses. These same bodies recognize that while privacy concerns are important, robust economic activity is dependent on the free flow of information. While the particulars of all these documents might differ, the basic thrust is similar — to protect data collected from individuals without inhibiting the flow of information. These initiatives are resulting in global convergence of legislation.

Recently, privacy legislation in many jurisdictions was extended to cover the private sector, and most recently, to not-for-profit groups that engage in commercial activities. For example, in 2010 Alberta's access and privacy commissioner's office recommended that a not-for-profit recreation facility comply with a request for information regarding an incident that resulted in a sports team being fined for the alleged misdeeds of one of its participants in the facility's bar. The privacy commissioner found that because the bar in the facility sold beverages to patrons, the facility was considered to be a commercial enterprise, and as such, was covered by the *Privacy Act*.[18] This is an example of "coverage creep" that will no doubt result in privacy protection in virtually all organizations.

Similarly, coverage creep has now moved legislation beyond simply enabling privacy commissioners to respond to complaints; in some jurisdictions organizations themselves may be compelled to report privacy breaches.[19] There are many ways that information could be exposed, such as by sending information via fax to the wrong number or through the theft or loss of a computer or hand-held device. Although privacy protection is expanding, there is considerable variation with respect to how broad the legislative mandate is in any particular jurisdiction and what powers privacy commissioners have. For example, some privacy commissioners have the ability to compel compliance with legislation, while others can only make recommendations and must rely on moral suasion. These differences notwithstanding, the trend is toward more robust legislation.

The concern for privacy and the development of privacy protection practices and legislation is a result of four interrelated factors: the first three are the result of technologies that make new forms of privacy invasion possible, while the fourth factor relates to the EU's directive. The first factor that has raised concern is that computers have improved the ability to store, retrieve, and transfer information. These improvements can lead to more efficient and effective services. The computer's capacity to improve the management of large volumes of information, however, also raises an important privacy question. Will unnecessary and irrelevant information be collected because of the computer's storage capacity? Ruth Gavison argues that the modern concern for the protection of privacy can be attributed to "a change in the nature and magnitude of threats to privacy, due at least in part to technological change." [20] In this regard, the Supreme Court of Canada notes:

> In fact, in our modern informational society, where intimate details of one's life may be available through computerized information accessible to many more persons than those initially entrusted with the knowledge, the security that information will be kept in privacy may be even more significant than one could have historically imagined. [21]

Privacy legislation can provide a foundation of rules and regulations to address these and other issues.

A second factor is the growing concern about government "data banks" or "data warehouses." Governments collect a dizzying array of information about individuals because of the nature and extent of the services they deliver, such as health care, social services, education, and licensing. An important privacy question is: Should comparisons of different databases through "data matching" be permitted in order to build electronic profiles of individuals? Should "data mining" be permitted to determine trends and patterns of behaviour? This ability to link different categories of information about an individual across departments or levels of government raises particular concern. These activities are also prevalent in the private sector. Data mining and data matching will be explored in more depth in the next section, but suffice to say at this point that privacy legislation governing the public sector is seen as an important way of keeping government open and accountable by allowing citizens some measure of control over what personal information their governments hold and for what purposes it is used.

A third factor that has led to the proliferation and convergence of privacy legislation is that elements of e-commerce are raising privacy concerns in relation to the Internet. Internet companies are creating devices to identify, track, and develop profiles of consumers. Consumers are concerned about the loss of anonymity, as well as the potential sale of their personal information to third parties for a variety of purposes. Internet companies include social networking sites. In 2007, the hugely popular Facebook began tracking its users' activities on third party websites and announcing these activities to the individual users' friends, as well as delivering ads relevant to those activities that featured the users' information.

Pause for a moment and think about that as a consumer: you make a purchase from a website that sells sex toys; this visit is announced to your friends on Facebook (which includes your mother, your work colleague, and your favourite teacher from grade three) and encourages them to consider buying a toy for themselves, as you, their friend, have determined this product is worthy of purchase. Although Facebook later changed this policy, its CEO announced in 2009 that privacy is a social norm from the past. Subsequent changes to Facebook's privacy practices made privacy controls far more complicated for the average user, just by virtue of giving the user more options for information dissemination control.[22] By 2010 Facebook had announced that it would be sharing its users' information with "pre-approved partner websites." Facebook's continued changes to its privacy practices have led its critics to charge that although users ostensibly have more power to control how much information is shared about them, few have the technical acumen to properly manage their privacy settings. The complicated case of Facebook will be discussed in depth in chapter 6.

A fourth factor contributing to proliferating and converging privacy laws is legislative as opposed to technological: the 1995 directive of the European Union discussed earlier in this chapter.[23] This directive raised the possibility of trade sanctions against countries with inadequate laws for privacy protection. To be a member of the EU, countries have to be signatories to the European Convention on Human Rights. This convention provides a right to respect for a person's "private and family life, his home and his correspondence" and has been broadly interpreted by the European Court of Human Rights. Because of its experience with Fascist and Nazi governments during the World War II era, Europe was exposed to atrocities inconceivable to most North Americans as a result of the unchecked use of personal data that exposed race, ethnicity, and sexual and political orientations. These experiences sensitized Europeans to privacy considerations, resulting in the development of strict guidelines for data processing; the 1995 Directive compels EU member states to terminate data flows to those countries that it deems are not sufficiently protecting data.

Privacy, then, is primarily protected through legislation worldwide that developed to some extent through "peer pressure" over the last few decades. Both the numbers of countries with legislation and the numbers of the sectors covered in legislation is increasing, as is the pressure to conform as a prerequisite for entering into trade agreements. At the same time global forces such as the threat of terrorism, the concern for security, and the proliferation of invasive new technologies are simultaneously eroding privacy regimes in many countries, such as Canada, Great Britain, the United States, and France. Predictably, a veritable industry has sprung up to promote the protection of privacy, including lobbyists and non-governmental organizations dedicated to the issue. The most visible of the latter is Privacy International, based in London and Washington. While free-flowing data is very good for trade, it can cause very real problems when used for purposes other than for what it was collected. These problems are the subject of the following section.

DATA FLOW, THE THIRST FOR INFORMATION, AND THE PROBLEMS OF PRIVACY PROTECTION

If the magnitude of data collected by retailers, government officials, and others is astonishing, the ability of new information technologies to facilitate the transmission of this information around the globe is even more so. This data flow is critical for commerce, but it is also important for other purposes, such as crime prevention. The different purposes of data flow create vexing problems for privacy protection, particularly for certain groups of people. Many corporations are multinational and thus personal information may cross borders as part of their routine business practices. This is often the case for national companies as well. For example, a local company might provide Internet connectivity, but the person providing technical assistance might be located on another continent. This person not only has access to the customer's account information but, through remote access to the customer's desktop, can often fix the problem virtually. As technology enables the easy dissemination of information and the distribution of both employees and those providing goods and services to the company on contract, the physical location of the company becomes increasingly irrelevant.

Once information crosses a border, however, it becomes subject to the laws in that jurisdiction. This practice first attracted notice in Canada when the province of British Columbia announced that it planned to outsource the management of BC medical information to an American company. Since the passing of the *USA Patriot Act* in 2001, in response to the 9/11 terrorist attacks, American companies are required to surrender information to the FBI upon request and are prohibited by the same act from revealing that the security of the data has been compromised. (The title of the act is in fact an acronym; the full name is the *Uniting and Strengthening America by Providing Appropriate Tools Required to Intercept and Obstruct Terrorism Act*.) Once the information has passed into the hands of the American government, there is no assurance that the information will be used only for the purposes for which it was collected, as the act allows for the possibility of other uses.

The problem with such an outsourcing situation quickly becomes clear. For example, an HIV-positive person living in Vancouver has no assurance that his medical information will not be given to the FBI or to US customs officials. As being HIV-positive was at one point reason to be denied entry into the United States, an HIV-positive Vancouverite could have been prevented from engaging in a popular weekend activity: cross-border shopping. If individuals cannot be assured that their personal information will be treated with the same respect for privacy as it is in their own country, it seems reasonable to ask whether such transfers should be permitted. The questions raised by privacy commissioners and others about data crossing borders resulted in the revamping of Canadian regulations for the contracting out of information management.[24] If it appears that the data are being used or disclosed inappropriately, there are problems with complaints and enforcement. Privacy commissioners are limited in their jurisdiction, and the scope of their investigations and enforcement mechanisms do not extend to other countries. The USA Patriot Act has created a plethora of other problems that will be discussed later in this chapter and this book.

A related issue for privacy protection is that of data matching. The combination of a variety of databases that contain personal information can be used to draw very detailed electronic profiles of consumers and citizens. Private sector records include such things as details of products purchased (what, when, how many), financial records, phone records, video rentals, books purchased from bookstores or borrowed from libraries, and detailed travel information. State records include an even longer list of information: taxes paid, charitable donations, property owned, vehicle registration, customs information relating to travel in and out of the country, immigration status, trial results and sentences, and forensic information gathered through law enforcement such as fingerprints and DNA records. Closely related to this is data mining, which involves using a set of automated techniques to extract information that is buried in large databases to determine patterns of behaviour. The resulting information that is drawn from "matching" and "mining" data can be used to produce a profile of the citizen consumer. These profiles can be used for relatively benign purposes, such as a government department trying to detect social service fraud or a store determining to which addresses a sales flyer advertising lawn furniture should be sent, or the more privacy-infringing activities of racial profiling or creating profiles of the "types" of people most deserving of credit or most likely to commit crimes.[25]

In the United States, terrorist prevention agencies make extensive use of data matching and data mining to determine who might be a terrorist and where vulnerabilities to national security might exist. While other governments, including the Canadian government, are not as enamoured of these techniques as tools in their counterterrorism arsenals, some do share information (such as passenger lists on airplanes) with the United States, which the US can in turn compare to data already in its possession. Profiling and data sharing are becoming increasingly popular methods of determining who is allowed to board a plane or cross a border. At best, these activities can be described as discriminatory because they place limits on personal freedom on the basis of someone's ethnicity or circle of acquaintances. At worst, inaccurate information can result in horrific consequences for innocent citizens. The infamous example of a thirty-four-year-old Canadian telecommunications engineer who was detained in the US while in transit home from an overseas vacation offers a frightening illustration of data sharing and profiling gone wrong.[26] Syrian-born Maher Arar was accused of having links to al Qaeda, and was eventually deported to Syria, where he was tortured and made to confess to attending an al Qaeda training camp in Afghanistan. He was detained for almost a year without being formally charged with a crime. The RCMP provided information to the United States that led to his detention and deportation; the RCMP had created an extensive profile of Arar through searching public documents that they then shared with their American counterparts. This background check included a rental agreement signed by someone suspected of al Qaeda links. After an investigation by a Commission of Inquiry, the Canadian government exonerated Arar, admitted to making multiple errors in this case, and paid $10.5 million to him in restitution. The American government, however, refuses to remove Arar and his family from its "watch list" that prohibits certain individuals from travelling though American air space.

Given the pressures of the global marketplace and the efforts of governments to work together to prevent terrorism and international crime, attempts to block transmission of personal information to other countries will be next to impossible. For this reason, privacy commissioners have focused their efforts on establishing legislation that outlines circumstances when transmission outside of the jurisdiction is permissible (e.g., agreements in place that provide for a comparable standard of privacy protection and audits to determine whether there are unauthorized uses and disclosures). In this way, privacy commissioners are able to investigate the activities of the body that discloses the information if concerns are raised about uses and disclosures in another country. That said, regulation of data that move from one jurisdiction to another can be very difficult, particularly given the competing demands for its use. The next chapter illustrates the complexity of the issue with respect to medical information.

Thus far this chapter has focused on information privacy — the flow of personal data that is collected, transmitted, and stored by organizations. This form of privacy is clearly emerging as one of the most vital. But it is not just technology or the propensity of organizations to collect data that threaten our privacy, it is also our willingness to exchange privacy for something else. Teenagers give up a measure of personal autonomy for the electronic leashes that their parents present to them in the form of cellphones. Being instantly available to their parents is considered a small price to pay for the ability to be instantly available to their peer group. The teenagers' parents relinquish control over their information every time they sign up for a loyalty card at their neighbourhood gas station or grocery store. Allowing a corporation to track their purchases and their movements for marketing purposes is considered to be a fair exchange for the reward points they collect every time they make a purchase. These points can be redeemed for yet more goods and services. In the marketplace, privacy appears to be a negotiable commodity, readily sacrificed to satisfy material desires.

What would seem utterly baffling to someone who lived a hundred years ago surely would be the readiness of people to reveal the most intimate details of themselves to a virtually limitless audience. This includes posting pictures of themselves in compromising situations (such as having had too much to drink) on Facebook, or posting YouTube videos of themselves engaging in activities that most people would consider very personal — squeezing a pimple, kissing, or defecating. Others go on syndicated television shows to confess to or denounce others for committing all manner of egregious behaviours. Or they might participate in a reality TV show. The premise of this TV genre is to track the behaviour of "ordinary people" in a variety of situations that will likely provoke intense emotional reaction (and therefore drama and sensationalism). As Andy Warhol predicted in 1968, "In the future, everyone will be world-famous for fifteen minutes." It would seem that those who willingly participate in these privacy-invasive activities are willing to do so to achieve Warhol's fifteen minutes of fame.

While those who participate in the aforementioned activities may not have thought through all the consequences of their actions, they are at least to some degree exercising free will when they engage in them. Many privacy advocates point out that the choice of privacy is the luxury of those who can afford it. The rich can purchase homes with high fences around them, while the poor are confined to multiple housing units with private living areas but shared common spaces. The rich can enjoy recreation in private clubs, while the poor play street hockey or kick the soccer ball around the field of the local school. The rich drive privately owned vehicles; the poor take public transit. Free will to protect privacy can be exercised to the degree that a person is both able and prepared to exchange it for some other good.

What is worrisome about the preceding examples is that

some people are forced to give up their privacy in order to gain access to something they need as opposed to something they want. The most obvious example of this is the ability of the poor to access social services. In order to avoid fraud, the state requires recipients of various forms of aid to provide an enormous amount of information which is then compared to other databases of similar information that can be accessed by a variety of service providers. In effect, the state keeps these people under surveillance in order to ensure that they are not earning income beyond a certain level or to determine whether they are living with a person of the opposite sex. Most middle-class taxpayers would object to the state stipulating what their living arrangements should be, or how many jobs they can hold, but welfare recipients are forced to comply with these intrusions into their personal affairs in order to receive state benefits.

In Canada, modern welfare practices evolved from those that governed the interaction between the federal government and indigenous people. As historian Keith D. Smith observes: "The importance of surveillance was well understood by those concerned with 'civilizing Indians' in the late nineteenth century."[27] The Department of Indian Affairs kept meticulous records on all aspects of the lives of its wards, including such things as what style of clothing particular Indians wore. These records were not compiled for the purpose of understanding the Indian way of life, but reflected and promoted the Euro-Canadian understanding of what comprised normality. "The underlying impetus of all this observation and intelligence gathering was to provide a portrait of the progress of colonial rule. It identified individuals and groups who were adhering to state policies, and singled out those who were not for further remedial discipline."[28] Feminist writers hasten to point out that it is not a coincidence that in the twenty-first century, those who are subjected to the most privacy-invasive practices are single women with children; much has been written about the state's imposition of restrictions on their behaviour in order to maintain morality. Once again, this is particularly true for minority women now and in the past. Smith notes that "in all spheres, the actions of women were placed under particularly close scrutiny in regard to restrictions on their movement. . . . The mission to impose patriarchal relations and the private/public dichotomy operative in non-Indigenous Canadian society was unmistakable."[29] Canada is not unique in this regard; privacy-invasive practices aimed at the poor, the marginalized, ethnic minorities, homosexuals, and women have a long history in countries around the world.

It is not just the poor who can be coerced with respect to relinquishing privacy, however. Employers and prospective employers subject workers to all manner of privacy incursions, from benign forms of interaction to outright surveillance. Privacy invasions start right at the point of hire. For example, the City of Edmonton in Alberta, Canada, requires applicants for city jobs (which are unionized with relatively high pay and benefits) to complete an online application process. Until recently, applicants were obliged to sign a form acknowledging that they have read the following: "Please be aware that the data you provide on this application form will be transferred to our electronic recruitment system, Taleo, hosted in the USA, and may be subject to U.S. laws."[30] The reference to "U.S. laws" meant that the information that a job candidate in Edmonton provides would be subject to the *USA Patriot Act*. As was noted earlier, it allows the US government access to any information that a US company might have, and to use this information for purposes other than for what it was collected. This might not sound like such a big problem — unless of course you happen to be an observant Muslim with the last name of bin Laden. Your dilemma becomes whether to provide the City of Edmonton with the voluminous information that is required in the application process, knowing that it might find its way into the hands of a foreign government who will use it for counterterrorism purposes, or for some other purpose. No problem — you have nothing to hide, right? But again, what happens if you coincidentally happen to share the same name and birthdate as someone else who is wanted on drug smuggling charges? What might happen the next time you fly to the Caribbean for a winter vacation and your flight stops to refuel in Florida?

Another invasive hiring practice comes in the form of employee assessments. One firm that specializes in these assessments claims: "Employee Assessments allow your company to understand and predict human performance and potential, ensuring you select the right person for the right job. They improve the quality and efficiency of your recruiting, qualifying, interviewing and selection processes, allowing you to make better hiring and promotion decisions and ensuring your employees will be a perfect fit in your company culture." [31] This is done through tests that ask questions in seven areas, including "personality, motivation, and culture fit." Obviously, questions that go beyond trying to determine job skills and experience will be far more detailed and invasive than simply asking for the last place a prospective employee worked. Whereas questions designed to assess such qualities as "judgment" were previously posed in a face-to-face interview, assessment now takes the form of multiple choice tests completed on a computer and sent to a third party for analysis. This third party may be a company located in another country. The dilemma job seekers face is that if they refuse to give up particular information, they are limiting their employment opportunities.

Once an applicant is actually hired, there are many forms of privacy invasions that he or she might be subjected to. Many companies require their employees to submit to random drug testing. A positive test could result in dismissal or suspension. While some drugs (such as alcohol, heroin, or crack cocaine) pass through a person's blood system within hours, traces of marijuana can remain in tissues for many months. Similarly, particular combinations of over-the-counter drugs can give false positives. Evidence of this is demonstrated at every Olympic Games when athletes are stripped of medals and an uproar ensues as to the validity of the test that showed them testing positive for a banned substance. In the case of an employee who fails a drug test, the implications are equally severe in that this form of dismissal can seriously compromise future employment prospects. The inclination, therefore, is for an employee who tests positive for drugs to keep the details of the incident as quiet as possible. Employees are also subjected to many different forms of surveillance while at work. New technologies are permitting companies to keep watch over employees when they are at home as well. These developments will be discussed in more depth in chapter 5, but suffice to say that surveillance includes the use of video-taping, the use of biometric identifiers (voice recognition, retinal scans, fingerprints) for security purposes, and the use of radio-frequency identification tracking devices. While all of these technologies have serious privacy implications for individuals, employees are theoretically not "forced" to acquiesce to them. But is there really any free choice if employees must by economic necessity continue to work for a particular company?

There are far more subtle ways in which an employee's privacy can be compromised but which nonetheless represent an incursion into an individual's personal space. A management tool that is growing in popularity is the "retreat," which is designed to break down barriers that prevent employees from engaging in collaborative creative thinking. The word *retreat* suggests safety — the removal of oneself to a place of safety and security where one can reflect on matters of importance. Retreats have in the past been used primarily for spiritual purposes and were solitary experiences wherein participants prayed, meditated, or reflected, sometimes in darkness. More recently, retreats have been used for so-called "team building." In these exercises, participants go to an off-site location to focus on issues that they do not normally focus on in their day-to-day work lives. Goals of organizational retreats typically relate to such things as strategic planning or improving communication; the achievement of retreat objectives requires the active participation of attendees. While some participants embrace the opportunity to share their thoughts and reflections with others, other participants may resent what they perceive to be an intrusion into their personal space. This can also be said about the "workshop," a similar exercise that requires participant interaction and exchanging information.

Students in educational institutions are being primed for these increasingly common workplace activities. More and more of their courses require them to post online blogs wherein they are required to publicly reflect on course themes and critically assess the blogs of other students. The difficulty with "reflection" with respect to privacy is that when we give serious thought or consideration to a particular issue in the social sciences or humanities, we do so from a perspective that is closely tied to who we are (for example, our gender, our social class, our ethnicity, our upbringing). Explaining our perspective might require that we share aspects of our personal lives that we are not comfortable with sharing in a professional context. This is particularly true if we think that our perspective could differ from that of the majority of the group and if we are not sure that the group will look kindly on a dissenting viewpoint. This discomfort must be measured against the possibility that our reluctance to participate will lead others to brand us as lacking collegiality or difficult to work with. As one former privacy commissioner observes: "There is considerable pressure on us in all aspects of our lives to be more open with everyone about our feelings and states of mind. In some quarters, to maintain a sense of privacy about aspects of one's existence is viewed as anti-social." [32] Even more troubling, of course, is that many instructors neglect to review the privacy statements of the blogging or social networking sites that they use; some sites require users to consent to the site using personal information in ways that some might find objectionable. Privacy-aware students will encounter additional problems when they enter the workforce; more and more companies are using electronic application processes for positions. Very few students understand the implications of their checking the "I agree" box on consent forms. Those who are aware may be graduating with a huge student debt and thus not in a position to choose not to consent (and by default, not apply for the job).

While the transmission of information facilitates trade and commerce, it can have grave consequences for the ability of individuals to control what others know about them. The appetite for our personal information appears to be insatiable, and various incentives are provided that make it seem reasonable enough to share it. The public lack of concern with the risks is undoubtedly also a consequence of the unequal impact of privacy invasion on particular people. Minorities, the poor, and those who are in need of support from the state are acutely aware of these issues in a way that the middle-class majority is not. As is often the case, those whose rights are the most threatened are the least equipped to defend themselves.

PRIVACY PROTECTION, PERSONAL AUTONOMY, AND CONTROL

The preceding discussion illustrates that threats to privacy come from many directions. These threats may be externally generated or may arise as a result of benign neglect through either ignorance or indifference. What is clear is that privacy is a complex concept with many dimensions. Notions of what properly comprises an individual's "personal" space are both culturally derived and evolving along with social norms. Though it might be difficult to define precisely how, it is clear that rapid technological change has dramatically multiplied and amplified the threats to privacy. Unfortunately, privacy is one of those things that most people do not think about too much until it is lost. As the Standing Committee on Human Rights and the Status of Persons with Disabilities observed:

> Classically understood as "the right to be let alone," privacy in today's high-tech world has taken on a multitude of dimensions. According to certain privacy experts, it is the right to enjoy private space, to conduct private communications, to be free from surveillance and to respect the sanctity of one's body. To the ordinary Canadian, it is about control — the right to control one's personal information and the right to choose to remain anonymous. *Privacy is a core human value that goes to the very heart of preserving human dignity and autonomy.* It is a precious resource because once lost, whether intentionally or inadvertently, it can never be recaptured.[33] (Emphasis in the original.)

But as with any resource in society, there are other interests that compete with privacy. Chief among these are national security, managerial efficiency, and social and political engagement. But it is the concept of transparency that trumps all competitors — this value is fundamental to good governance. As such, transparency's close companion, access to information, must be balanced with privacy, just as the interests of the individual are frequently weighed against those of the larger community in other political debates. Access to information and its importance to the development of a good and just society are the focus of the next chapter.

CH_3
Freedom of Information
(FOI)

TRANSPARENCY FOR THE PUBLIC GOOD

The protection of personal privacy is attracting considerable attention in Western democracies because of the ease with which information circulates on the Internet and the adoption of potentially intrusive new security measures to address international terrorism. In contrast, less attention is paid to freedom of information, but this does not mean that FOI is not of equal importance. It is recognized worldwide as a crucial component of a democratic state because transparency helps to expose corruption, ensures due process in law, and encourages the citizen engagement that is central to political participation. For newly emerging democracies, the concept of "open government" challenges previously accepted notions that the interests of society as expressed through the power of the state take precedence over the interests of individual citizens. These countries often use access to information legislation as a means for their societies to both confront and reconcile past human rights abuses. The ability to access information, however, necessitates the restriction of privacy. While protection of privacy is a critical component of safeguarding the well-being of the individual, access to information is a critical component of the accountability regimes that underpin functioning democratic societies with market economies.

This chapter's focus is on FOI as it relates to citizens and their governments, because these accountability regimes are for the most part confined to accessing information held by the state. The chapter begins with a discussion of the relationship between transparency and good governance, and overviews the development of FOI regimes globally. It then moves to an analysis of how transparency is operationalized in legislation and administrative practice in the public sector, with a particular focus on the administrative structures and processes that impede the adoption of the culture of openness. While the focus of this chapter is on transparency and accountability in the public sector, much of what is said in this regard can be applied to consumers who obtain goods and services from private or non-profit entities. Corporate and non-profit leaders do not have to worry about being re-elected, nor do customers/clients have the same rights of access to information as citizens. But corporations and non-profits still have to maintain the confidence of their clients and their shareholders. In addition, they must abide by the regulatory framework that governs their industry. Accountability is key to good managerial practices, and as we have seen in previous chapters, there is a close relationship between transparency and accountability.

What ultimately separates the public from the private

and non-profit sectors is that the public sector's purpose is to promote societal interests through the provision of certain goods and services that are deemed too important to be left to the private sector. Citizens cannot "opt out" of being a citizen unless they move to another country and renounce their citizenship. While an unhappy customer can stop buying a product, an unhappy citizen does not have the right to stop paying taxes. As such, a citizen has certain rights vis-à-vis the state that a customer does not have vis-à-vis the business that she patronizes. Currently, access to information held by organizations in the private and non-profit sectors is limited to information pertaining to the individual making the request. In contrast, legislation relating to requests for access to information held by the state allows for far more expansive requests, as citizens have the right to know how the public interest is being defined and how state resources are being allocated. Predictably, this raises an important question to keep in mind when reading the following discussion of FOI: How should the desire of an individual, business, or other organization to keep information private be reconciled with the claim that releasing the information is in the public interest?

There are two components that underpin the right to FOI that together define the relationship citizens have with their government: (1) individuals should know what personal information is held; and (2) they should have the ability to "see" what the government is doing in order to hold it to account. The first component relates to the protection of an individual's right to privacy. In order to protect this right, citizens need to know what information the government holds that pertains to them personally, and they should be able to correct it or request that extraneous information be deleted.

The ability to exercise some control over information that is in someone else's possession allows individuals a degree of sovereignty over their public identity. Because this form of access is integral to an individual's privacy rights, access and privacy should not be conceived as always in opposition to one another. The second component concerns the ability of citizens to access information that does not pertain to them personally; it provides the focus of this chapter.

The reason that citizens should have access to government information is simple: they need information in order to exercise their democratic rights in a responsible manner, and as taxpayers, they paid for its collection and retention. The types of information in which citizens might have an interest are as varied as their purposes for requesting it. Applications for access to information can be made at all levels of government. For example, at the municipal level, a reporter who became ill after an evening dining out requested health inspection reports from Toronto Public Health for all city restaurants for the previous two years. This led to a year-long series of newspaper stories in the *Toronto Star* on the safety of city food establishments. In response to the ensuing "Dirty Dining" scandal, Mayor Mel Lastman ordered a four-month crackdown on restaurant inspections that resulted in a hundred charges being laid and sixty restaurants closing.[1] At the provincial level, a citizen in British Columbia was concerned about the reorganization of the province's ferries and asked the premier's office for all the background reports and analysis that contributed to the cabinet decision. He successfully argued that this decision had been the focus of much public debate and that the public was concerned that government decisions were increasingly being undertaken without sufficient public scrutiny, particularly with respect to government outsourcing and privatization of services that require significant expenditures of public funds.[2] At the federal level, a reporter from the *Globe and Mail* made an Access to Information request to Public Works and Government Services Canada for records regarding the money that had been spent on the federal government sponsorship program since the 1994–95 fiscal year. This $40-million-a-year program was supposed to support cultural and sporting events but in fact comprised an aggressive advertising campaign in Quebec to promote Canadian unity. It was eventually revealed that, in addition to providing government funding for commercials, hot air balloons, and festivals in Quebec, advertising firms were overcharging the federal government for their services and in turn making donations to the Liberal Party of Canada. These revelations resulted in the so-called Adscam scandal, and in the next election the formidable and long-serving Liberal government was reduced to a minority in Parliament.[3] While these examples are drawn from three different levels of government, they all demonstrate how an individual request for information can be made in the name of "the public interest"— specifically, in order to hold government to account.

The determination of whether the right to access is deemed more important than the right to protection of privacy is about the relative importance of group rights versus individual rights, the public interest versus private autonomy. It should be noted, however, that "the public interest" is a contested concept. An individual or a group of individuals might make claims for information in the name of "the public interest" while the state might deny access based on claims of protecting "the public interest." It is thus more useful to think of claims for access to and protection of information as products of competing societal interests struggling to define what they perceive to be the public interest.

The ability of an individual to retrieve information held by the government is fundamental to the legitimacy of the state. That is, in a democracy leaders lead because others are prepared to follow them. We give leaders authority by electing or appointing them to a particular office using accepted practices that are clearly delineated. We trust them to act on our behalf because they have convinced us in an election that their ideas and their character make them deserving of the responsibility that we give them. In a perfect world, this trust is based on a continual assessment of their performance in office. The politicians who shape government are not only responsible for their own actions, they take responsibility for the policy decisions made by their party and for the actions of public servants who implement government policy. Periodically we are asked to renew the mandates of our elected representatives; we either re-elect them or choose someone else to represent us. We monitor these decisions in light of the alternative choices that could have been made. While accountability is less direct in other sectors, leaders who lose the confidence of employees, boards of directors, or clients often find it difficult to maintain their positions of authority.

Leaders lose legitimacy and eventually authority when their followers become disenchanted with their actions, but if unpleasant truths or contentious decisions are kept from the electorate, the electorate will remain blissfully ignorant. Leaders will therefore continue to stay in power even if they are doing things that are not promoting the "public good," however the public good is defined. So, for example, FOI allows citizens to request information regarding the travel and entertainment expenses of politicians and bureaucrats. This may reveal that the taxpayer is paying for visits to strip clubs or for the use of escort services. FOI might also reveal that government contracts are consistently awarded to family members of cabinet ministers. The ability to obtain information helps us to ensure that leaders are exercising the power we have given them in an appropriate manner, one that is consistent with the collective wishes of the electorate. In this case, "an appropriate manner" means a manner that falls within the parameters of the authority vested in the offices these leaders occupy. It also refers to a manner that is consistent with what the majority of the electorate believes is the best course of action with respect to policy choices. But citizens can make this determination only if they have access to information regarding decisions that have been made or if opposition parties or the media have access to it and are thus able to bring issues to the public's attention.

The preceding observations are not limited to a particular nation-state; they also have relevance to international relations. Transparency has often been associated with the twentieth-century notion that openness will foster international stability and peace. This idea arose in reaction to the secret treaties that were signed prior to the outbreak of World War I that many pointed to as the cause of the war. While it is acknowledged that privacy has a place in the negotiating process, it is now accepted that the results of negotiations should be open and accessible. As the world became more economically integrated after World War II, international bodies began asking for statements of account for audit purposes. These are referred to as "compliance information regimes."[4] So, for example, countries must submit information about changes in trade policies to the World Trade Organization. Arms control or disarmament treaties require verification that the signatories are actually doing what they say they are doing.

Increasingly, transparency is also being demanded in financial markets. Global financial transparency helps to expose terrorist networks, arms dealers, drug traffickers, tax evaders, and money laundering. But the benefits can be more mundane; transparency also facilitates the production of comparable corporate information that is useful for investors and their agents as they engage in securities trading. Since the 1980s, the ideology of "small government" and limited government intervention in the marketplace has ruled the day. Recent financial scandals and the 2008 stock market plunge precipitated by the sub-prime mortgage crisis in the US has lent credence to those who claim that complex investment vehicles must be put under tight regulatory scrutiny.[5] These events also support the view that transparency (in the form of more audit requirements and supervision as well as greater regulatory integration) would improve risk management. As with accountability, the desire for transparency is thus not confined to governments: rules have been developed to create access to information regimes both in the private and the public sector. It can be expected that access to information will soon extend its reach to the non-profit sector, particularly given the size and influence of many international non-governmental organizations.

At the outset of this section, it was argued that the ability to access information is critical for good governance. It also was asserted that the determination of whether or not information should be released is the result of competing interests, which often pit a collective right — namely, the right to access information in the interest of the public good — against the individual right to keep information private. As with privacy, the recognition that information sharing is critical to democratic societies is not a new phenomenon. The next section discusses the evolution of FOI regimes and their regulative counterpart: access to information legislation.

THE MARCH TOWARD REGULATION

Commentators point to Sweden's 1766 *Freedom of the Press Act* as the world's first attempt to secure the right to disseminate information through the auspices of freedom of expression.[6] Given that this act placed restrictions on criticism of the state, it would take another fifty years for the Swedish act to be amended to such a degree that it actually could be described as protecting freedom of expression. More recently, it was at the global governance level that the desire for free-flowing information was articulated. On 14 December 1946, during its first session, the United Nations General Assembly passed a resolution calling for an international conference on freedom of information. Resolution 59 (1) opened: "Freedom of information is a fundamental human right and is the touchstone for all freedoms to which the United Nations is consecrated." Two years later, the Universal Declaration of Human Rights was adopted. Article 19 affirms "the right to seek, receive and impart information and ideas through any media and regardless of any frontiers."[7] Access to information can thus be seen as a natural progression emanating from those states that embrace freedom of expression and free presses.

The constitutions of many former eastern European and Latin American countries provide explicit constitutional protection of the right to information. With the exception of Sweden, Norway, New Zealand, and Portugal, the constitutions of most liberal democracies in the industrialized north do not, although the right to access has been inferred in a variety of court decisions. Similarly, the European Convention on Human Rights (1953) does not provide an explicit right to access to information, but it does contain other provisions through which access can be obtained. In *McGinley and Egan v. the United Kingdom*, the European Court of Human Rights ruled that under Article 8 (family and private life) members of the British forces who witnessed experimental atomic explosions had a right to information pertaining to the effects of those explosions on the health of those involved.[8]

Sweden and Finland passed the first modern *Access to Information Acts* in 1949 and 1951 respectively. The United States followed in 1966 with its own legislation. In most countries, the catalyst for the adoption of a FOI act is not democratic enlightenment but political partisanship or scandal. In the case of the US, a Democrat-dominated Congress sought information about a Republican executive. Later, the act was strengthened because of the Watergate break-in, eventually leading to the resignation of President Nixon. Nonetheless, the 1960s was a decade wherein a variety of American civil society groups demanded rights (civil, women's, and consumer, to name just a few) and the importance of freedom of the press to democracy was recognized. In the early 1970s, Denmark, Norway, the Netherlands, and France adopted access to information legislation. Australia and New Zealand followed suit in 1982; Canada's law came into effect in 1983.

A second wave of countries passing access to information acts occurred with the fall of communism; by the 1990s having such legislation was considered fundamental to democratic governance and became an international norm endorsed by various supranational bodies. Ukraine and Hungary were the first countries from the former Soviet block to pass a FOI law in 1992; most of the central and eastern European countries now have access laws. The adoption of access to information regimes in newly emerging democracies that are trying to reconcile a past filled with human rights abuses poses difficult questions, given the files on citizens that were compiled by secret police and the fates that often befell citizens as a result of those files. Security forces acquired much of the damning information from friends, neighbours, or relatives of the person profiled. Some fear that allowing open access to these files will cause major damage to friendships and to families. There are many different ways that countries have approached this issue, from completely open access to providing limited access for the purposes of preventing those involved in human rights abuses from serving in the current government. It is interesting to note that three of the four former eastern bloc countries that were included in the Open Society Justice Initiative's fourteen-country study of access (Bulgaria, Romania, and Armenia) consistently rank as top performers in compliance, beating out such countries as France and Spain.[9]

Like the former Communist countries, many Latin American nations are grappling with human rights issues in connection with the gruesome fates of those who "disappeared" during the era of military dictatorships in the mid-twentieth century. These unfortunates were tortured and murdered by security forces, and their children were often handed over to military families for adoption, only to discover their true identities many years later, as adults. While Mexico was not a military dictatorship during this era, it has had similar issues of human rights abuses. It passed its access law in 2002, the same year President Fox ordered all files that detailed human rights abuses to be declassified.[10]

Mexico continues to grapple with serious human rights abuses, many in connection with the *maquiladoras*, manufacturing and export assembly plants that lie along its border with the United States. In the northern borderlands of Chihuahua, hundreds of the poor women and girls employed in these sweatshops have been raped and murdered, their bodies found mutilated; hundreds more have simply disappeared. The drug wars — armed conflicts among Mexican drug cartels, which supply illicit drugs to the United States — have also contributed to Mexico's poor track record in the area of human rights. Law enforcement officials are criticized for being, at best, indifferent and inept and, at worst, corrupt and complicit in drug trafficking and other criminal activities. Those who attempt to determine who is perpetrating the crimes may find themselves becoming victims. Recently, representatives of the United Nations and the Organization of American States joined Mexico's National Human Rights Commission in criticizing the government for failing to protect journalists against corrupt public officials and drug traffickers, especially along its northern border. Attacks, murders, and disappearances have earned Mexico the reputation as one of the most dangerous places in the world for a reporter to work.[11] Security issues are also a problem for law enforcement officials working to combat the drug cartels: in

December 2010 the last remaining police officer who served the border town of Guadalupe disappeared.[12]

In Mexico and elsewhere, the hope that access to information laws would help in the fight against government corruption was a significant factor in their adoption. Belize, Trinidad and Tobago, Jamaica, Columbia, and Peru already have access legislation. The most recent South American country to pass FOI legislation is Chile; this followed a successful 2006 court challenge by a Chilean environmental group claiming that the American Convention on Human Rights guarantees a right of access to information. The international tribunal's ruling sets a precedent for other courts that access to government-held information is a right.[13]

In Africa, South Africa, Zimbabwe, Angola, and Uganda now have access legislation. There is a difference, however, between having such a law and actually using it for its intended purpose. For example, Zimbabwe claims to have modelled its *Access to Information and Protection of Privacy Act* (2002) after Canada's, but its act has been cited as the source of increased power of the government over the press and the suppression of free speech. Ironically, as a consequence of Zimbabwe's act, independent newspapers have been shut down and journalists have been jailed. Paraguay and Serbia's laws also have been criticized for restricting free speech and the dissemination of information.[14]

An interesting contrast is the case of South Africa, whose act began as severely oppressive but has evolved into the world's strongest and most progressive — at least on paper. Under the apartheid regime, the government controlled all public information and the channels through which that information flowed. Like Zimbabwe's act, South Africa's

Protection of Information Act of 1982 worked directly counter to the spirit of FOI legislation in that it gave the government the power to regulate information that it regarded as "sensitive." It enabled the government to shut down a number of newspaper outlets and to curtail the publication of any information that the government deemed inappropriate for mass consumption. As one critic commented:

> The information made available for public consumption was simply meant to brainwash the public and also entrench its political agenda of discrimination, segregation and separate development to create an uninformed, ill-informed and unenlightened society. The ultimate intention was simply to safeguard its unpopular and infamous regime.[15]

The mid-1990s saw a complete reversal in South Africa when the right to access records held by both private and public bodies was enshrined in Section 32(1) of the *Constitution of the Republic of South Africa Act* of 1996. Constitutional protection of the right to access information is unusual, and it signals the importance that South Africa places on FOI for building a democratic nation that embraces equality. The subsequent passage of the *Promotion of Access to Information Act* of 2000 operationalized this right.

The following year, South Africa passed another law that linked FOI and human rights. This law was the result of four years of lobbying by the Open Democracy Campaign group, a coalition of human rights, legal rights, social justice, environmental, church, and labour groups. The coalition argued that FOI is critical for ensuring corporate and government accountability. Its website cites the observations of the 1998 winner of the Nobel Prize for economics, Amartya Sen, who argues that "information is crucial to development and the prevention of disaster." As Sen points out, democracies that guarantee freedom of the press have never suffered through famine: "A free press and the practice of democracy contribute greatly to bringing out information that can have an enormous impact on policies for famine prevention. . . . A free press and an active political opposition constitute the best early warning system a country threatened by famine could ever have." [16] While South Africa is moving in the right direction in its quest for administrative openness, it should be noted that implementation of the law is quite another story: South Africa rated quite poorly in a fourteen-country survey on request compliance conducted by the Open Society Justice Initiative. While laws can be passed and even enshrined in constitutions, in order to change an organizational culture from one of secrecy to one of openness public officials must be adequately trained in implementing those laws. [17]

The uncovering of systemic corruption and government waste over a twenty-year period provided the impetus for the Japanese FOI law, which took effect in 2001. A dozen other Asian countries also have similar laws, including Hong Kong (1995), South Korea (1998), Pakistan (2002), India (2005), Taiwan (2005), and China (2008). For developing nations, part of the incentive for passing a FOI law is that countries wishing to receive money from supranational organizations like the World Bank or non-governmental organizations have to comply with the regulatory framework laid out for them. Access to information is part of this regulatory framework.

The UK (2005), Switzerland (2006), and Germany (2006) were laggards among the world's democracies in adopting FOI acts. The passing of access legislation garnered little attention from the German media, perhaps because access to the files held by the East German secret police had been opened to the public over a decade earlier. In contrast, the passing of the UK legislation was accompanied by much fanfare, as it was considered a major victory by its advocates. They argue that the legislation will provide a strong antidote to the "culture of secrecy" that they claim dominates UK public affairs. As in many other countries that adopted FOI legislation, the hope is that increased transparency will result in the restoration of public trust in government.

By 2006, over fifty states had access to information legislation,[18] and another dozen were working on it. But more than one hundred countries still do not have laws, including countries such as Brazil, Libya, Democratic Republic of Congo, Vietnam, North Korea, Venezuela, Cuba, and all of the Arab Middle East with the exception of Jordan. Russia, Argentina, Nigeria, and Kenya are working toward drafting legislation. Unfortunately, the 2001 attacks on the World Trade Center and the Pentagon had a dampening effect on the march toward greater transparency. Just as a spate of countries were embracing the concept of openness in government and implementing their own legislation, the United States was once again distinguishing itself as a leader. This time, however, it separated itself from the pack by withdrawing its commitment to both FOI and protection of privacy. Only six weeks after the terrorist attacks, the USA *Patriot Act* was passed, effectively trumping transparency and privacy protection values with measures aimed at enhancing security.

These actions caused a ripple effect throughout the world, with many other countries passing legislation that followed the lead of the USA *Patriot Act*. While the commitment to FOI appears to be waning, no country has actually repealed its legislation.

Though the context and details of access legislation varies among countries, the general outline remains fairly similar. Similarly, since World War II there has been a steady march worldwide toward passing access legislation. Legislation that promotes transparency, however, does not guarantee openness. The next section describes the basic characteristics of a FOI regime and the challenges inherent in implementing "open-government" administrative practice.

ADMINISTRATIVE PRACTICE:
CHALLENGES TO THE CULTURE OF OPENNESS

Access regimes worldwide share similar assumptions and features. The basic premise is that governments do not "own" information; they are simply its custodians. The information ultimately belongs to citizens; FOI articulates citizens' rights to it in the absence of compelling reasons not to grant access. These rights are set out in laws and usually apply only to citizens or permanent residents of any particular country. Access regimes provide clear and reasonable timelines for providing this information. As such, the laws impose a duty of compliance on the part of public officials. There are exceptions that might prevent disclosure, but these must be clearly articulated in the law and it is up to the public body to justify the exemption. Typically, exemptions seek to protect public welfare or safety, commercial secrecy, or individual privacy. In cases where there is an identifiable harm that will result from disclosure, the harm must outweigh the public interest. In case of a dispute, an independent arbiter will make the decision regarding whether information should be disclosed or not. In recent years, FOI has been extended in countries such as South Africa to cover private organizations that provide public services.[19]

In a federal system, each level of government has its own access legislation that applies to its various departments. In both federal and unitary systems,[20] local government bodies are covered by the same acts that cover the government that delegates authority to these bodies. Access legislation varies, however, with respect to its application to regulatory boards, commissions, panels, agencies, and government-owned corporations. Critics of exemptions to such legislation argue that access laws should apply to any organization that serves the public interest and is in large part funded by the government. There is, however, no definitive formula for defining what constitutes "the public interest" or at what level of funding a government should be assumed to be influencing organizations to such a degree that they should be considered an extension of that government. While government-funded corporations can legitimately claim that business secrets must be protected from competitor scrutiny, critics complain that the problem of releasing information that might play into the hands of the competition could be handled by specific as opposed to blanket exemptions.

Limiting access to information can also be crucial to the workings of government itself. There are good reasons for a veil of secrecy shrouding government caucuses and, in particular, decision making at the level of senior committees or the cabinet. Secrecy can, for example, allow decision makers greater room to manoeuvre when negotiating deals. Restricting access to certain information can also aid consensus building. This is particularly important in parliamentary systems, which rely in large measure on party solidarity. Once a bill is before parliament, all the members of a party are expected to vote the same way on the bill. If a majority of party members vote against bills proposed by their own government, the government may face a vote of non-confidence and, should it lose such a vote, be forced to resign. This can encourage party leaders to keep potentially sensitive information to themselves and can have the net effect of inhibiting open debate in parliament among members of the same party. Instead, debates happen behind closed doors, and the face that is shown in parliament, and to the public, is one of solidarity. In contrast, in republican systems, such as that of the United States, party discipline is much weaker. Although, in any system, political parties are seldom eager to expose their divisions in public, congressional representatives are held more individually accountable for the ways in which they vote: they feel a greater pressure to vote according to the wishes of their constituents, as opposed to the wishes of their party. Prominent individuals and special interest groups can thus have considerable influence on how a representative votes. Members of Congress are, moreover, expected to defend their own positions in open debate; they cannot shield themselves behind the argument that they must support their party's platform on an issue. The resulting lack of consensus can also make it more difficult to get a bill successfully through Congress, but it also produces a degree of transparency in the legislative process that is not generally found in parliamentary systems.

In the case of a dispute over a bureaucratic decision to withhold information, an independent third party passes judgment. This could be a court, a panel, the public service ombudsman, or a commissioner, whose duties may be limited to issues of access or may include both access and privacy. Some FOI commissioners serve as arbiters who have the power to issue orders. Other commissioners act in the capacity of an administrative ombudsman: they investigate a complaint and then issue a recommendation to the head of the institution that is the subject of the complaint. While some might argue that a commissioner who can only advise the government to do something lacks clout, in reality the commissioner's advice, like that of an ombudsman, carries significant moral weight, which can be quite forceful when combined with the power of the press to disseminate the details of the conflict. Moreover, the role of an advisor, as opposed to that of an arbiter whose decisions are binding, opens the door to a more co-operative relationship with public servants, who are more likely to work with a commissioner to find a solution that will satisfy those who lodged the complaint. Either way, access commissioners' powers of investigation are considerable: they typically cannot be denied access to a record, and interfering with an access investigation is considered a criminal offence.

But a regulatory regime does not guarantee that a culture of openness will replace a culture of secrecy. Passing new laws designed to ensure access to information and protection of privacy may do more harm than good if those who develop and implement new compliance policies and procedures use them for nefarious purposes or, as is more often the case, do not have a sound understanding of the fundamental objectives underlying access and privacy legislation. The end result can be the development of absurd access policies that reflect the defensive posture of the unsure, who instinctively default to the position of refusing a request for information. For example, some universities require the coordinators of academic programs to seek permission from the registrar in order to obtain access to lists of students that these administrators need to perform their jobs. Public trustees may be denied information by their counterparts in other provinces, information that would enable them to locate relatives of deceased people — despite the fact that few people would object to being contacted by a trustee if they are entitled to receive money from an estate. Public health authorities have refused to tell parents whether or not paramedics gave a child a tetanus shot while providing first aid at the scene of an accident. Not only do such overly rigid interpretations of access policy undermine administrative efficiency, but they can also have very unfortunate consequences for people who need access to information but cannot get it in a timely fashion.

Misguided interpretations of the law and its underlying principles are not, however, the only reason that requests for information are sometimes denied. Unfortunately, as the implementation of FOI laws becomes routinized, so too does the ability of officials to sidestep the laws and to justify their actions for doing so. One could even speculate that conscious efforts to suppress information have contributed to the malaise currently affecting liberal democracies, in the form of declining trust in government and citizen disengagement.[21] Governments everywhere are straining under multiple burdens: increasing loads of debt, the complexity of governance, and global forces that increasingly work to limit the power of the individual state. Special interest groups, journalists, opposition politicians, and others have become adept at using FOI laws to access information that will help them further their own agendas. In response, government officials, seeking to defend the status quo and safeguard their positions, may attempt to restrict access, although they might take exception to the idea that they are simply trying to "hide" information from citizens. From their perspective, they are protecting what they regard as the public good from those who seek information in order to pursue goals that, in official eyes, may not serve the interests of the majority. Ultimately, however, the default should be to bring the debate out into the open, where all parties have an opportunity to state and defend their positions.

As has been well documented by Alasdair Roberts, organizations have a great capacity to resist change and maintain the status quo, especially with respect to implementing access to information rules.[22] This can be done through direct challenge or through passive resistance that effectively diminishes the impact that FOI laws have in practice. Transparency requirements can affect record keeping in a number of ways. They can, for example, encourage people who control information and make decisions to be overly cautious with respect to what they commit to paper. There is no right to information that is not contained in a written record. Thus, one of the fundamental tenets of a functioning bureaucracy may be obviated: a paper trail that allows an observer to determine on what basis a decision was taken. As Roberts notes, this trend is evident within the Canadian public service. Whereas in the past public servants wrote notes, now there is a tendency to keep written communication to a minimum so as to reduce the material available that some-one might legally request — material that could be "FOIPed."

If it is known that information will be publicly available, there is a tendency to be more circumspect with respect to what is said and, in particular, to what is written down. An interviewer in a public sector hiring process will not likely commit to paper that a candidate's mannerisms, miniskirt, and revealing neckline gave her the appearance of someone applying for a job at a strip club rather than as a policy analyst. Instead, a vague reference to "professionalism" might be made. Similarly, a professor writing a student's letter of recommendation for a publicly funded scholarship is unlikely to note that the applicant has serious anger management issues that might pose a danger to faculty and other students. Instead of a candid assessment, the professor is likely to provide subtle clues that something is amiss that will hamper academic success. Sparse and cryptic note taking is attributable not only to a conscious decision to minimize what FOIPed notes can reveal, it is also a result of the increased pace, volume of written records, and complexity of public management that has not been met with a commensurate increase in resources. There is danger that a gap will emerge between the formal decision-making process that is duly noted in a written record and the undocumented, informal decision-making process that arguably becomes more important. This is not to say that there is never any type of record of this decision making; it might be contained in numerous email strings. What may be missing, however, is a summative record that explains how and why the decision was made.

Other administrative practices that diminish transparency are not followed consciously. This is particularly evident with respect to inward transparency, specifically, the ability of the person outside an organization to navigate its administrative structure. Email has changed the nature of communications — it is now more informal than before. This can be seen in the change from the use of official memos done in triplicate with names, titles, and departments duly noted. Now a request to an organization is often answered by email or by a form letter that is not signed by the sender. If it is signed, it might contain a first name, but frequently senders do not bother to include their last name, their position, or their contact information. A phone call to an office is handled by an automated answering system, and it can be very difficult to navigate to the appropriate place in order to talk to a "real" person. This is particularly frustrating for a requestor of information who may be told that the department they have contacted does not have the information in question but is not then directed to the appropriate place. The net effect of these administrative practices is to decrease transparency and obscure the lines of accountability.

Perhaps the biggest indirect challenge to transparency is attributable to a lack of resources. Legislatures may pass laws, but not much is likely to change unless a considerable sum of money is dedicated to the implementation of the new laws. Public administrators need to be trained not only in the basic principles of FOI but also in the processes and procedures for dealing with access requests. Without this training, administrators will default to the "keep it a secret" position. In its fourteen-country study, the Open Society Justice Institute found that even in countries with FOI laws, 38 percent of requests were simply ignored. Of the requests that were denied in writing, 60 percent were refused for reasons that were not recognized in law. The study also offers numerous examples of arbitrary practices that thwart efforts to access information, such as security guards denying someone entry into the building where an access request must be filed or public officials refusing to take a request from a person simply because, in their estimation, the person does not need access to the information.[23] Clearly, even the most well-designed regimes will fail if inadequate resources are put into the professional development of those who are expected to implement the new rules.

Other challenges to transparency are more direct, such as destroying or falsifying records. These events typically come to light as high-profile scandals such as the tainted blood affair in Canada in the 1980s or the Somalia affair of the 1990s. In both cases records of discussions among public officials regarding how to manage the serious problems that had come to their attention were destroyed shortly after the investigating commission requested them. In response, Canadian FOI legislation was modified to make it an offence to obstruct the release of information by hiding, changing, or destroying a record.

Some direct challenges to FOI entail regulatory or legislative change. As such, they are visible and can attract considerable public attention. A typical change in parliamentary democracies has been restricting access to records of cabinet and other bodies that deliberate policy decisions. Another effective measure that decreases access is increasing fees for information requests and appeals against decisions to deny access. Roberts has written about how successful these tactics were in decreasing access to information in two Canadian provinces.[24] He also notes that, in Ireland, increasing the rate charged for making access requests and appealing decisions to the information commissioner had the effect of halving the number or requests.[25] As noted earlier, in the wake of the 2001 terrorist attacks, the United States increased restrictions on access to information. Other countries, including Canada, followed suit. Executives in both countries also issued directives to their public services that encouraged officials to adopt a narrow interpretation of FOI legislation. Both initiatives resulted in court challenges.

The centralization of the processing of requests that are deemed by ministers to be of a sensitive and potentially politically damaging nature is yet another challenge that inhibits true transparency. For example, a request for a record that contains information that is likely to create controversy will be flagged and dealt with by officials higher up in the bureaucratic chain. Testimony at Canada's Gomery Commission hearings revealed that ministerial staff from all governments and Department of Communications officials routinely met to discuss media strategies in order to have an appropriate one in place before the release of information. This does not mean that the information was not released — just that certain information, or information requested by particular people, was delayed.[26] Similar problems were noted in Alberta; the overt political interference with a 2004 Alberta access to information request by a reporter who wanted to see flight logs resulted in the RCMP becoming involved. At issue was how the premier and other Conservative Party MLAs were using taxpayer-funded airplanes. Departments have thirty days to comply with FOI requests in Alberta; as in other jurisdictions, they may take a lot of time to process requests because they simply lack the resources to make a timely response. But journalists or opposition politicians who request information as part of a policy debate need the information in a timely fashion. A delay could render the information irrelevant if the "moment" to contribute to shaping a policy has passed. In this case the information was requested in June; the government provided the information three days after the November 22 election.[27]

The idea of taking a proactive stance against the release of sensitive political information was taken one step further by the Irish. Some departments released the information requested by one journalist to other journalists known to be sympathetic to government. Certain departments actually posted details (including names) of requests and requestors on a website. Cited as an advance in transparency practices by the proponents of these changes, these actions were decried by detractors as a method of discouraging journalists from asking for information, as the "surprise" element with respect to the information requested was destroyed.[28] Similarly, an overly enthusiastic response to a FOI request has the same effect; releasing vast quantities of information can be used to delay critics who must wade through a pile of insignificant information to find what they are looking for.

A final but critical factor in decreasing transparency is the restructuring and outsourcing of government service provision. While restructuring the administrative state, outsourcing and privatization are lauded as ways to increase operating efficiencies and to save money, these reforms are in fact rooted in neoliberal ideology, which favours reducing the size of the state by moving many of its activities to the private sector. This is a problem for transparency and for accountability more generally. As a result of the move in the 1980s to "smaller government" and governments that would "steer" the ship of state as opposed to providing the rowing to get there, many services that had previously been delivered by a particular government department were contracted out to service providers outside of government or privatized outright.[29] In their quest to "work smarter" and be "leaner," many governments restructured their public service departments and strove to eliminate task duplication. As a result, some services now are delivered across multiple departments, with each department responsible for a particular task. This has resulted in tremendous administrative confusion with respect to where the lines of accountability run. It is often not clear who is responsible for what, both from the vantage point of the citizen and from the perspective of a public servant. If a requestor is not sure who is actually accountable for a government service, that person will have a difficult time directing an access to information request to the appropriate department.

The use of Internet technologies was lauded as a cost-saving device in keeping with the "leaner" government philosophy; individuals could access information online and communicate instantly (and cheaply) without having to go through an intermediary. But this, along with the desire to cut costs, often resulted in the removal of the support personnel that kept the records in order.[30] The volume of electronic information is huge and thus, one assumes, would assure a good paper trail. But the ability of people to retrieve the information on demand in many cases has been greatly reduced. As was pointed out earlier, having the information does not guarantee that you can find it when you need it.

The difficulties with privatization and contracting out for

maintaining administrative accountability are even more complex and have been documented elsewhere. To summarize briefly, once a service passes into the private sector for provision, the rules and norms that govern administration in the public sector no longer apply. As Mulgan observes:

> Because contracting out confines the duty of contractors to the performance of the terms of contracts and confines the right of supervising principals to enforcing the terms of contacts, it rules out the possibility of day-to-day supervision and intervention which is part of the normal practice within bureaucracies and indeed within any organisation of employees serving a common employer.[31]

Moreover, ombudsmen working in the public sector typically do not have the jurisdiction over the private sector that they would need in order to investigate maladministration.[32] With respect to information access, contractors fear that providing detailed information regarding their operations and contracts will undermine their competitive position. While one part of the argument for outsourcing involves avoiding the costly "red tape" that characterizes bureaucracy, the "red tape" itself comprises part of what makes a bureaucracy an indispensable organizational form. That is, a bureaucracy is critical for governments wishing to provide services that are not based on the ability to pay but rather on notions of equity tied to citizenship. Access to information may be part of the bureaucratic baggage that is openly disparaged as a characteristic of the public service, but it also indispensable in ensuring that citizens are treated fairly and equitably.

Lest the preceding give the impression that resistance to transparency is always a bad thing, it should be pointed out that there are a number of reasons why transparency might not always be the best mode of operation. From an organizational perspective, transparency will illuminate best practices and will encourage "good behaviour." But the problem with transparency is that it might potentially open the floodgates of unsorted information. If released information is not assessed and packaged as part of a manageable framework, it could result in information being taken out of context and providing an incomplete and thus inaccurate version of any particular situation. To counter this, public servants may resort to deception in order that a particular "truth" is not used in a way that creates confusion or in a way that distorts situations.

Moreover, there are compelling reasons for policy makers to retain a degree of privacy when contemplating decisions. As was noted earlier, privacy allows for dissenters to dissent without fear of having the differing opinions spun as a sign that junior ministers or policy makers have lost confidence in or respect for their superiors. With respect to decisions that require negotiations, a public body may be able to defend an outcome in the end that has clear benefits, but it may not so easily be able to defend sacrificing particular interests during the negotiating process in order to achieve those ends. There is also the danger that complex policy may be reduced to simplistic treatments by either special interest groups or by the media. Complex problems require sustained analysis by those with specialized expertise; this by definition would take decision making out of the hands of most members of the general public. Another central tenet of bureaucracy is the guarantee of anonymity. The politician makes the decision and is responsible to the public for that decision. Each public servant involved in the implementation of the decision is responsible to his immediate superior for his performance; at the top of the pyramid the senior bureaucrat remains shielded from the public, as she is accountable to the minister. This system is critical to ensure that the public servant performs a specialized function within the bureaucracy on the basis of his expertise, as opposed to his political acumen or partisanship.

This leads us back to the beginning: transparency must be balanced against privacy. Though the public may wish to know all sorts of things, it may be for the wrong reasons. Publishing salaries of public servants may be useful in assessing how well public tax dollars are being used, but it may also discourage competent people from applying for public sector jobs. Will the average person make serious assessments on salary versus the relative "worth" of a particular position, or is he just curious as to what his neighbour the public servant makes? Thus, in all access to information regimes, the public interest must be weighed against what the public is interested in, and this determination must be made according to clearly articulated rules and within established timelines. Finally, how the public interest is defined is dependent on the values of the particular society in question.

INFORMATION ACCESS, EQUITY, AND FAIRNESS

Like protection of privacy, FOI is a complex concept — one that can be difficult to explain to a neophyte and complex to operationalize. Access to information is fundamentally about transparency — and transparency is a necessary condition for accountability. Yet the point at which transparency becomes an infringement on the ability of individuals or a group of individuals to pursue their self-interest without undo interference from others is not clear. Trade-offs have to be made, and the tolerance for negative consequences will depend on the value the society puts on those things being traded. This point is particularly relevant for those who work within the administrative structures of large organizations. Developing access to information policies without understanding basic principles will result in cumbersome procedures that will more often than not diminish both accountability and administrative efficiency. But clearly the assessments of the pros and cons of any particular course of action can only be made if the concepts are unpacked, the consequences are clear, and a value weighting is made.

While FOI legislation is applicable to the public sector, much of what has been said about the importance of transparency also holds true for the private and non-profit sectors. The fundamental difference between them is that the private sector seeks to maximize profit for its shareholders while the public sector seeks to maximize the public good for its citizens. The non-profit sector sits somewhere between the private and public in that it also focuses on maximizing a public good, but that good is generally targeted at a subset of the public. The concern for accountability and ethical practices runs through all sectors, however, and ultimately stakeholders in any of them can hold decision makers responsible for their actions. Again, the linkage between access and privacy is evident, as privacy legislation that covers the private sector ensures that individuals have access to personal information held by corporations. While non-profits are unevenly covered under privacy legislation, in some jurisdictions they fall under private sector legislation if they engage in commercial activity.

Access to information regimes are based on a number of fundamental principles: individuals have the right to know what is known about them; the rules for what can be accessed and what cannot are clearly laid out; organizations have a duty to comply within a reasonable time frame; and a third party has the responsibility to act as an arbiter in case of dispute. While these rules do not guarantee a culture of openness, they at least signal the commitment of an organization to the basic principles of accountability. Of equal importance to a culture of openness is adequate training for those who will be implementing the rules, as lack of compliance can often be traced to inadequate understanding of proper procedure as opposed to outright refusal to fulfill a given request. Accountability is a prerequisite for good governance, but there are no easy answers for how it should be attained and how much should be expected. What is clear, however, is that the electronic age is ushering in a whole new set of issues that must be grappled with in order to ensure that structures of government align with some basic democratic principles. Specifically, how we handle information has much to say about how we approach notions of personal autonomy, equity, and fairness. How these combine to produce good governance should be of central concern to anyone who values democratic institutions. The next three chapters demonstrate the complexity of balancing access to information with the protection of privacy by analyzing "real life" applications of the two concepts.

CH_4
Sharing Medical Information:
Antidote or Bitter Pill?

THE SPECIAL CASE OF HEALTH INFORMATION

The preceding chapters on access and privacy illustrate the complexity inherent in balancing competing societal interests. Transparency in organizations is clearly desirable from an accountability perspective. In government, it ensures the rule of law — that is, that legal principles and regulations are understood and followed. While specific laws could arguably favour a particular group, at the very least the rules are visible and can therefore be debated. In all sectors, organizational transparency thwarts corruption. The ability to get information not only facilitates good governance, but it is also increasingly important from a market perspective: it allows companies to target selected consumers with advertisements for goods and services. At the same time, privacy is an important societal value. Privacy allows a measure of "self-autonomy" — the ability to control what is known about oneself. A related concept, confidentiality, is also important.

In the corporate world, "company secrets" — the ability to keep certain information under wraps — allow businesses to compete in the marketplace. Similarly, in government, secrecy is sometimes necessary to national security.

What becomes obvious is the complexity of the application of access and privacy concepts to the management of information and, more generally, to the management of societal interests that balance the rights of the group vis-à-vis the individual. This chapter is the first of three case studies that looks at what happens when the "rubber hits the road" with respect to the application of theory to real-life situations. This first case study discusses the management of health information. The health care sector is one where the benefits of sharing information are readily apparent, but it is also one in which the information is considered to be very sensitive. Two critical facets of medical information management will be examined. The first is the management of health information through the creation of an electronic health record (EHR); this brings the question of the optimal balance between access to information and protection of privacy into stark relief. The benefits to health care providers and their patients of having instant access to information are obvious, as are the risks to privacy that are embedded in systems that store personal information in electronic databases. A second facet of medical information management is the use of data derived from large populations for use by the medical research community to promote health. Using health information for this purpose is secondary to the purpose for which it was collected. As such, careful consideration needs to be given to the balance between the benefits that society will derive from using this information for the purpose of health research and the possible harm that might be done to an individual whose health information is shared. What EHR and health research have in common is that both must concern themselves with confidentiality and the informed consent of those whose information is being shared.

The management of medical information more generally, however, is an excellent example of the challenges associated with balancing the interest of individuals in controlling their personal information with the benefits that may accrue to society when this information is shared. In cases where medical information is used (often by private sector companies) to prevent insurance fraud or to curb substance abuse, transparency and accountability are only loosely related to broader social benefits. Increased access to medical information by those who provide medical services and do research, however, promotes the larger common good by creating efficiencies in health care delivery and in advancing our understanding of diseases and other health issues. While innovations like the EHR provide the paper trail so critical to organizational accountability, the primary goal of the EHR and medical research is to improve the treatment of medical conditions.

ELECTRONIC HEALTH RECORDS

The EHR is most easily understood as the systematic collection and digitization of a patient's health information so that anyone who treats that patient in a variety of health settings has electronic access to the patient's medical information. This includes such things as immunization status, laboratory tests, radiology images, and billing information. There are major benefits to information sharing in the medical field.

The collection, retention, and sharing of medical information can facilitate the diagnosis and treatment of an illness, it can save the health care system money by eliminating duplicate tests, and it can prevent instances of fraud such as patients seeking multiple prescriptions for narcotics. For example, a college student who visits a campus medical clinic with a sore throat and feeling sick with the flu might be tested for strep throat by a physician who also orders blood tests from another facility. The student is feeling tired, so she goes home to bed, forgoing the blood test. Two days later, her condition has deteriorated and she is taken to the emergency room of a nearby hospital. The attending physician calls up her medical file on a computer, sees that the strep throat test is negative, has the blood work done, and gives her painkillers for her sore throat. Having her medical information on hand provides the physician with her history, including test results with the click of a mouse. This is particularly useful if the patient is too sick to communicate this information effectively. Easily accessible medical information prevents the duplication of the strep throat test and the quick diagnosis of mononucleosis from an analysis of the results of the blood test. In addition, entering the information pertaining to the painkiller the student was prescribed prevents her from leaving that hospital and visiting another medical facility to get a duplicate prescription for the narcotic. Proponents of the type of EHR that facilitated information sharing in this example promote it as a tool that will enhance patient safety as well as increase the efficiency and effectiveness of treatment.

Health information, however, is a very sensitive form of personal information. It can include such items as a patient's mental health diagnosis; a laboratory test result indicating that a person is a carrier of a sexually transmitted disease; payment information related to a cosmetic medical procedure; or a prescription for pharmaceuticals taken by women in relation to their reproductive health. Genetic information is a particularly sensitive form of health information. It raises unique concerns about privacy and health information because:

- test results may reveal sensitive health information about other family members,

- validation of test results may require information about other family members,

- a small amount of material may reveal a large amount of information,

- genetic information may be used by insurance companies and employers with possible negative consequences for individuals,

- genetic information may reveal "family secrets" such as paternity issues and adoption, and

- genetic testing must respect the right "not to know."

But even routine health information that is collected or created in the health care sector every day is private and personal. As such, the management of health information is of particular interest to privacy advocates.

As in other areas, privacy rights need to be balanced with other valid objectives. As the authors of a report on health data systems point out, "privacy is not and cannot be an absolute in a democratic society." They argue that the public disclosure of certain personal information will always be necessary for the "protection of individuals and society" and that competing interests must be balanced. "That the claims to privacy and choice in personal disclosures are especially high and important in the health care field does not mean that they can, or should, always prevail over all competing interests."[1] For example, consider a university student living in residence who is very depressed and is seeing a school counsellor. University officials, such as the counsellor or a residence official, who have reason to believe that the student is at risk of suicide are allowed by legislation to contact the student's family members to alert them to their concerns, regardless of the student's desire for privacy.

Another competing interest with regard to privacy of medical information is public safety. The question of balance between the public's right to know and the privacy of the patient is particularly vexing in this instance. When does "safety" shade over into "convenience" for law enforcement officials who are investigating a crime? Clearly, emergency hospital staff reporting to police the injuries of a child whom they suspect has been abused by a parent relates to the safety of that child. Similarly, a psychiatrist reporting a mentally ill client's desire to return to the high school he was suspended from for the purpose of killing staff and students comprises an instance where safety is a vital interest. But what about the police requesting blood samples from the drivers of the vehicles involved in a car accident to determine if either was driving under the influence of alcohol? Should these records be provided to an insurance company to assist in its investigations and determination of liability?

These are just some of the issues that are raised by the

digitization and centralization of medical records that provide medical practitioners with easy access to the information essential for their work. But the EHR also contains information that other professionals argue they need for the same reason. Everyone having access to the same information will facilitate the most efficient and effective patient treatment. The trick, of course, is delineating how the claim for the information balances against the need for patient-practitioner confidentiality.

PRIVACY AND CONFIDENTIALITY

The particularly sensitive nature of health information has resulted in the development of policies, codes of practice, laws, and regulations to address privacy and, in particular, the confidentiality and security of such information. The policy rationale behind laws protecting health information is based on its personal nature, the negative consequences that could arise from inappropriate access to it, and the stigma associated with certain health conditions. In addition, the effectiveness of the patient–health care provider relationship depends in large part on the patient's expectations around the privacy, confidentiality, and security of the information that the patient shares with his health care provider. The Supreme Court of Canada describes personal health information as "information that goes to the personal integrity and autonomy of the patient," as well as information that is almost always communicated in a context that gives rise to the highest expectation of confidentiality.[2] Personal health information is imbued with a sense of both a right to privacy and an expectation of confidentiality.

It is clear that society values the fostering, maintenance,

and preservation of confidentiality with respect to personal health information. The Hippocratic Oath requires physicians to swear that "whatsoever I shall see or hear in the course of my profession ... if it be what should not be published abroad, I will never divulge."[3] The basic assumption that information provided to a doctor will not be disclosed to others unless express consent is given is the foundation upon which a trusting relationship is built. If that trust is not there, a patient may decide not to seek health care, or may withhold important information that is critical to the diagnosis and treatment of a medical condition. The basic tenets of the Hippocratic Oath are echoed in a variety of professional standards and laws, such as the Code of Ethics of the Canadian and American Medical Associations, the Ethical Principles of Psychologists of the American Psychological Association, and within subnational bodies like the College of Physicians and Surgeons of Ontario.

The importance of medical information is reflected in the wide range of laws that cover health information access and privacy. Health care workers are required to report to the government agency in charge of motor vehicles any medical conditions that might affect the safe operation of a vehicle by someone applying for a licence; child care providers and teachers are required to report suspected neglect or abuse to social services; and occupational health and safety legislation protects the privacy of injured workers whose employers would like to see their medical files. In addition, many jurisdictions have laws regulating particular health professionals that include provisions for handling health information. In Canada, the provinces of Alberta, Saskatchewan, Manitoba, Ontario, and Newfoundland have passed access to information and protection of privacy legislation specific to health information. Efforts to codify best practices into law reflect the sensitivity of this information and the fact that it touches virtually every aspect of an individual's life. But these also reflect technological advances wherein increasingly personal information can be gleaned from an individual's medical records that can be disseminated quickly and easily.

The disclosure of medical records has been a particularly contentious issue in sexual assault cases. If the complainant had been seeing a therapist, lawyers for the defence often have an interest in gaining access to psychiatric records, in hopes of discrediting the complainant's credibility on the grounds of mental instability or a history of sexual promiscuity. In a leading Supreme Court of Canada case, *R. v. O'Connor* (1995), the court ruled that such records could be disclosed to a judge if the applicant could make a convincing argument, without actually seeing the documents, that these records were relevant to the case. The judge would then decide whether the complainant's right to privacy outweighed the importance of the records to the defence. This decision struck down the so-called "rape shield" law, which denied the admissibility of any records that related to the sexual activity of the complainant as evidence. In 1999, however, the courts upheld revisions to the Criminal Code that limited the circumstances under which a complainant's personal counselling records could be disclosed.[4] Similar debates have occurred in the United States. The issue here concerns where the line should be drawn between the complainant's right to privacy and the defendant's right to access information that might be relevant to the case.

An interesting twist on the right of individuals to expect that their medical records will be kept confidential is a similar right of access to their own medical records. Privacy laws contain provisions that give individuals the right to look at the information about them that an organization holds. They are allowed to correct obvious errors, or in the case of a dispute as to the veracity of the record, they can insert a disputing note. But in some cases, providing an individual access to certain information might be damaging. For example, should a psychologically unstable individual be given access to records that might set off a psychotic episode? Should an individual be told that the person he thinks is his father does not share his DNA?

In previous chapters, it was noted that notions of privacy are both culturally specific and epoch-sensitive. This is especially true with respect to certain medical conditions, particularly those related to sexual activity, such as contraception, abortion, or giving birth to a child out of wedlock. The use of contraception and abortion are not only deeply personal issues, they are illegal in many countries around the world and tightly controlled in others. Both were illegal in North America until the 1960s. Though not a "medical issue" as such, adoption is a consequence of a woman's decisions regarding her reproductive health and is part of her medical history. It is also a good example of how shifting cultural norms affect the confidentiality of certain medical records.

In years gone by, a woman in North America who bore a child out of wedlock brought great shame to her family. Often she was sent away to give birth to her baby at an undisclosed location in great secrecy. As such, the idea that eighteen years later the adopted child might find her and expose this family secret was terrifying. Similarly, adoptive parents sometimes refrained from telling the adopted child that they were not his birth parents in an effort to spare the child the humiliation of knowing that he was a "bastard." While certain non-identifying information might be made available (such as that the father was a diabetic), laws from that era ensured that adoption records were sealed in order to respect the privacy of the various parties.

As the stigma attached to adoption decreased in North America, so too did the necessity for secrecy, and access to records opened up. Given that both parents and adopted children might still prefer anonymity, legislation was passed in various jurisdictions that allowed information to be released and/or contact to be made with the consent of both parties. Passive registries were set up, wherein interested parties can be connected if both join the registry and indicate they would like to make contact with their parents/child. A disclosure veto allows a name to be released to the parent/child if the other party indicates that he wishes to have his name released. Similarly, a contact veto allows a name to be released without consent, but prohibits contact. These measures reflect the generalized change in attitudes toward adoption in North America and the changing norms in handling the medical records associated with it. In other countries attitudes differ dramatically, and so too will the handling of these types of records.

The adoption issue puts into stark relief the conflict between the rights of the individual to privacy and the rights of the parent or child to information. The latter is particularly important to children, whose interest in making contact might be motivated more by questions about genetic or medical histories than a desire to know who their parents are. The issue of adoption records highlights the competing interests with respect to the access to or protection of medical information and also illustrates how attitudes toward the balance between access and privacy vary by epoch and by culture. Attitudes toward out-of-wedlock pregnancy within minority groups in North America may also differ dramatically; however, those groups must conform to legislation that reflects the majority's will.

At the international level, influential organizations such as the World Medical Association, the World Health Organization, and the Council of Europe have produced documents that highlight the importance of confidentiality of patient information.[5] These documents also recognize that patients have a corresponding right of access to their health information. Similarly, regarding the United States, Westin and van Gelder conclude:

> Now is the time for those involved in current health IT developments to develop a specific mechanism for balancing interests in a new electronic health data network. Achieving balances that a majority of the American public, as well as the health care community, can embrace as the best possible (though never perfect) system will be vital to the future development and operation of any future national electronic network.[6]

While this statement articulates the lofty objectives of using information communication technologies to facilitate the sharing of information to improve health care, the same types of concerns have been raised in the health community with respect to the health profiling of particular groups. Data matching provides an abundance of information about a patient that could lead to particular assumptions being made that could affect a diagnosis or the prescribing of a drug. Thus it might be assumed that an Irish Catholic is an alcoholic; a gay man engages in casual unprotected sex; an Aboriginal person has a poor diet; a Chinese person uses opium; or an elderly married woman is unlikely to be HIV-positive. This phenomenon is similar to that of racial profiling, which is discussed in more depth in the next chapter.[7] The possibility that extraneous information could inadvertently prejudice diagnosis must be considered in any discussion of the development of systems to manage health information.

There have been numerous complaints to privacy protection oversight bodies concerning employers collecting more medical data than they needed for a particular purpose (e.g., a doctor's note saying that a person had a medical condition that prevented him from working for five days is sufficient; a diagnosis of the medical condition is not required). Some employers have instituted drug testing for employees; these tests provide employers with medical information that indicates the presence of particular substances in blood or urine. The Canadian Human Rights Commission has ruled that this is acceptable if the employer can demonstrate that there is a bona fide occupational requirement.[8] That is, it is acceptable if the employer can demonstrate that the worker is in a safety-sensitive position, or if there are reasonable grounds to suspect the existence of an underlying problem that is impairing an employee's ability to meet the requirements of the job or is the cause of an accident, or if an employee has disclosed a current or previous drug or alcohol dependency issue. These criteria were applied to a complaint brought before a privacy ombudsman involving a school division that wished to compel student athletes to undergo random drug testing as a condition of participation. In this case, the ombudsman ruled that students had the same rights to privacy as adults. As the school could not demonstrate that any of these criteria applied, the policy was abandoned.[9] In this case the privacy rights of the students (as with the workers) were deemed to be more important than the risk to society if drug or alcohol use went undetected.

Another important area of concern with respect to medical information is genetic discrimination, which occurs when a person or group of people is disadvantaged by virtue of genetic makeup. A life insurance company might use genetic information to determine an applicant's likelihood of dying prematurely because of an inherited predisposition to an illness. Employers might use genetic profiling to determine a candidate's suitability for a particular kind of work. What is at issue here is that these determinations are based on evidence that is often contestable and sometimes purely speculative. In 2001, the U.S. Equal Employment Opportunity Commission sued the Burlington Santa Fe Railroad on behalf of railroad employees for administering blood tests that were used in an attempt to determine the employees' genetic susceptibility to carpal tunnel syndrome. These tests were illegal and their purpose was hidden from employees. In a blatant attempt to avoid compensating those who suffered from this syndrome, the tests were undertaken in the hope that a genetic predisposition to the disability would be determined, as opposed to addressing the repetitive and stressful conditions that the railway's critics claimed was the real cause of the disability. As one critic of genetic profiling observes: "These aspects of genetic surveillance, privacy, and discrimination are certain to persist as insurance companies and employers continue to press for legal access to genetic information." [10] The predictive aspects of genetic information have clear benefits, but they have the potential to create new forms of discrimination as well.

Although medical information is a particularly sensitive form of personal information, most individuals are prepared to share it with the appropriate health care personnel. It is shared with the expectation that it be kept in confidence. It is when an individual's medical information is shared for purposes other than medical treatment that sharing becomes contentious.

SECONDARY USES OF MEDICAL INFORMATION

The use of information by an organization for a purpose other than that for which it was collected is referred to as "secondary use." Typically, it is not practical for secondary users to collect information themselves; they rely on primary health care providers to collect and share this information. Often the person whose information is being shared is unaware that there is a secondary use of her data. Access and privacy legislation specific to the health care sector was developed in part because of the multitudes of legitimate secondary uses of health information. By law, in instances where consent is required, it must be "informed" consent. Those who are asked to provide data for a particular purpose must have a clear understanding of why the data are needed and also what the implications are of giving their consent. Clearly, if express consent to share is not deemed to be required, the conditions in which that sharing can happen must be limited and clearly delineated.

The secondary use of medical information is a major issue for the health care community and for privacy advocates. A variety of people may have an interest in health information, even though they did not collect it. For some, this information relates to their core activities — as in the case of health insurers and medical researchers. Others, such as an employer or a school, might also require medical information. An employer might need to accommodate absences from work owing to illness or make allowances for a worker's inability to perform certain tasks because of a medical condition. Similarly, a student might have a medical condition that impedes his or her ability to learn or to participate in physical education classes, or that requires absences from school, or that might necessitate emergency care. This information can be collected directly from the worker or the student, but, in certain circumstances, employers and schools have the ability to obtain it directly from the health care provider without consent. As always, the right to privacy must be weighed against the importance of this information to others.

Health Research: Consent and the Public Interest

One of the most important secondary uses of medical information is research. Health-related research takes a variety of different forms, including the impact on health of such diverse things as the environment, lifestyle choices, hereditary factors, education, and consumption patterns.

Governments typically promote health research; great savings can be realized in terms of reduced pressures on health care and social service systems, as well as reduced economic losses due to illness-based absences from work. Research gives public sector bodies insights as to where money is best spent within the health care, education, and labour systems in order to effect the largest benefit in improving the health of a particular population. Governments can provide support by funding research, but they can also support research by providing access to information for the purposes of conducting research.

Given the societal benefits that can be realized by research based on large populations, it is generally accepted that the consent typically required for the secondary use of personal information can be overridden by the public interest. Obtaining the consent of each individual contained in a particular database would be extremely burdensome for the researcher, or impossible if the person has died or has moved. Moreover, using only data from those who give consent will skew the study because all of the participants are self-selected. Researchers hasten to point out that the insights derived from the research not only benefit society, but will also benefit individuals either directly in terms of their own health or indirectly as members of a society that will use funds more efficiently. While this section focuses on health research, similar arguments are made in other disciplines.

Large quantities of information about a particular person can be gleaned by combining various data sets collected by various professionals — the school nurse, the chiropractor, the ambulance attendant, or the physician, for example. This information can be very useful in research that strives to identify causes of medical conditions or determine the best treatments. It is also very useful to drug companies for marketing their products. The use of secondary data greatly reduces the costs to the user because the data have already been collected. While the purpose might be noble in the case of medical studies, few people are comfortable with teams of researchers poring over their comprehensive medical histories and then possibly publishing information that could be linked to them. Typically, health information can be used for research once it has been stripped of identifiers that link it to a particular person.

The problem arises when researchers want to gather information about individuals from multiple sources in order to create a comprehensive picture of the subjects of their research that can be used to link health determinants to health status. Linked data are also useful for conducting cohort studies that follow particular individuals over time, as their information will need to be updated during the course of the study. In addition, these data are also useful in studying the spillover consequences of policies. So, for example, a policy that would reduce expenditures in one area may have the unintended consequence of increasing expenditures in another area. Linked information from medical and non-medical databases can be extremely useful in determining these relationships. What is needed, however, is a common identifier that can link the data: this element is typically is a health insurance number or name. These common elements, unfortunately, also match the data to an identifiable individual. Any researcher who wants to use data for a secondary purpose and who wishes to use matched data must provide compelling reasons to oversight bodies for doing so. Understandably, it is far easier to gain access to data that have been stripped of identifiers than it is to gain access to linked data. The latter is frequently approved for some health researchers as well as for researchers in other fields, such as historians seeking access to census data.

The confidentiality of research subjects is governed not only by legislation but also by research ethics boards and the bodies that provide research funding. In Canada, the Tri-Council (the Medical Research Council of Canada, the Natural Sciences and Engineering Research Council of Canada, and the Social Sciences and Humanities Research Council of Canada) provide oversight through directives to those researchers undertaking studies that involve human subjects. Researchers must assess privacy risks and threats to the security of collected information and follow approved procedures to protect and dispose of data. Universities that receive funding from the Tri-Council must adhere to the policies and procedures it sets out; otherwise funding will be terminated. As such, university researchers conducting any research (even those that are not Tri-Council funded) must have their studies involving human subjects approved by their university's research ethics board before beginning the study. As will be demonstrated in the next section, however, these oversight mechanisms are a recent phenomenon.

Health Research: Classification, Profiling, and Discrimination

Health research has long attempted to classify certain populations by genetics determined in part by race. Advances in genetic sciences and the advent of computer modelling support these classification efforts and promote the curative potential of disease-related genetic research. This has led to the claim that the future of medical research lies in the discipline of genetic epidemiology — the study of the causes of inherited disease in populations.[11] While these claims are welcome news to those suffering from an illness and waiting for a genetic cure, there are many who are much less optimistic.

To begin with, racial classifications are contested, as the notion of race itself is a contested concept. Both anthropologists and sociologists have long held that race and ethnicity are cultural and sociological constructs, and many biologists and geneticists are now coming to similar conclusions. In June 2000, when two distinguished scientitsts, Francis Collins, of the National Human Genome Research Institute, and Craig Venter, of Celera Genomics, unveiled a draft sequence of the human genome in a Rose Garden ceremony at the White House, Venter stated emphatically that "race has no genetic or scientific basis."[12] From this perspective, there are more genetic differences among members of a given ethnic group than there are among the groups themselves.[12] Medical research that focuses on genetic makeup tends to ignore the socio-economic, cultural, and environmental determinants of disease. Not only does a focus on genetics funnel thought in a particular direction, but it also fuels fear of the construction of racist and discriminatory categories that are grounded in faulty biological assumptions.

These fears are rooted in racist and discriminatory medical practices and in the crimes that have been committed in the name of medical research. In the nineteenth century, the supposedly scientifically based doctrine of "racial hygiene" was prominent in Europe and in North America. This doctrine was based on a crude misconstruction of Darwin's theory of evolution, claiming that some human lives were superior to others and that only the fittest would survive. Those who were poor demonstrated their lack of fitness through their failure to thrive economically. This thinking was applied to entire populations of people, resulting in hierarchies of human groups wherein particular groups were deemed to be racially inferior. This conception of the inferiority of groups was the justification for such practices as segregation in the United States, apartheid in South Africa, the "final solution" to the "Jewish problem" in Germany, and the "ethnic cleansing" of the Tutsis by the Hutus in Rwanda.

In the medical field, the notion of racial hygiene led to the emergence of eugenics, the "science" of improving a race by controlling the reproductive capacity of those deemed to be genetically inferior through forced sterilization. In the US, vasectomies were forced upon the criminally insane. The Canadian provinces of Alberta and British Columbia passed sterilization acts in the 1920s for the purposes of preventing mental "defectives" from reproducing. Until the abolition of these acts fifty years later, almost three thousand Albertans and four hundred British Columbians were sterilized. For most, this occurred without their consent and for reasons that were not based on genetics but rather on social class, ethnicity, and gender.[13]

It was Nazi Germany, however, that took the concept of eugenics to unprecedented levels. Eugenics provided the rationale for euthanasia, the "mercy killing" of those who were deemed unfit to live. The concept of *Deutsche Volksgemeinschaft,* or the community of the German people, obliterated personal autonomy and with it the ethical dimension of medicine. Those who were handicapped, deformed, mentally ill, afflicted with chronic illness, alcoholic, or regarded as genetically inferior on the basis of race or sexual orientation were considered candidates for death in order to provide for the collective health of the national community. Eugenically based justifications for extermination of the Jews have been attributed to professional opportunism: during the economic depression that preceded the rise of the Nazis, jobs within the medical profession were relatively scarce. Many Jews were doctors, and eliminating them as competitors for positions opened up opportunities for non-Jewish doctors.[14] Those German physicians who opposed Nazi ideology were forced to emigrate or were killed. It would be another fifty years before the German medical profession engaged in an intense process of self-reflection regarding its role in Nazi atrocities. This medical fraternity saw itself as elite but fundamentally altruistic, as opposed to secretive and misguided. Contemplation of its past history brought to the fore the relationship between transparency and ethics.[15]

The general acceptance of eugenics in the last century highlights the danger of using scientific justifications for discriminatory practices and explains the unease of minority groups with respect to large-scale research projects that use medical information for the secondary purpose of determining patterns of diseases. This case also demonstrates the necessity of developing moral and ethical codes for those conducting medical research. First and foremost in these codes is the notion of informed consent; this consent underpins personal autonomy and self-determination. Consent has its legal basis in a 1914 case in the United States, *Schoendorff v. The Society of the New York Hospital*,[16] in which the judge proclaimed that a surgery performed without consent constitutes an assault for which the surgeon is liable. But decades later, prisoners in Nazi concentration camps were subjected to all manner of experimental medical procedures in the name of research. The horrible deaths, disfigurement, and disabilities that the prisoners suffered as a result of these abuses led to the establishment of the Nuremberg Code, which outlined ethical principles guiding the use of humans in experiments.

It would be almost two decades later before the principle of informed consent would take hold, however. The impetus in the US came as a result of an article published in 1966 in the *New England Journal of Medicine* that outlined twenty-two cases of unethical research in that country.[17] These included the deliberate infection of residents with hepatitis at the Willowbrook State School for "mentally defective" children without providing adequate information to their guardians in the 1950s, and the injection of live cancer cells into patients at the Jewish Chronic Disease Hospital in the 1960s without their knowledge (and hence without consent). But it was a forty-year study conducted by the US Public Health Department of the consequences of syphilis for African-American men that provoked a wholesale rejection of previous practices in experiments involving human beings. The Tuskegee study began in 1932 to study the natural course of the disease in hundreds of impoverished Alabama sharecroppers. Shortly thereafter penicillin became the standard for treating syphilis, but subjects were not provided with this information and were prevented from accessing treatment that was available. The premise of the study was that syphilis had different outcomes for whites and blacks, and while this race-based hypothesis was debated, the fact that humans with a potentially fatal disease were not treated with a known and effective treatment did not raise ethical concerns. In addition to the obvious issues relating to having a life-threatening disease that was not treated, many partners of the research subjects were infected and their children were born with congenital syphilis. The project finally ended in 1972, after a long-time critic went to an Associated Press reporter with the story. A few years later the US government agreed to an out-of-court settlement with the subjects and their survivors.[18]

The lasting legacy of the Tuskegee study is American minorities' mistrust of public health projects and the proliferation of conspiracy theories, including that of AIDS being a form of genocide created by whites to eliminate blacks.[19] There are many other examples wherein particular groups in society were exposed to risks in the name of research. These serve as cautionary notes to those who claim that the risk that research poses to individuals pales in the face of the broader human benefits that research produces. Clearly, those who bear the burden of the research may have a different perspective than those who benefit from it. Ultimately, those who conduct medical research must keep ethical considerations at the forefront of the inquiry, focusing on individual autonomy and informed consent as key values. While the societal benefits of data collected from a large-sample population are huge, these benefits must be carefully considered against the possible harm to an individual within that population.

The fine balance between individual rights and societal rights in public health is particularly evident in countries like Canada. Using the Ottawa Charter for Health Promotions produced by the World Health Organization in 1986 as a foundation, Canada began to move away from the individualistic understanding of the impact of lifestyle choices as a key determinant of health toward one that highlighted the social context in which the individual lives. This emphasis shifts the focus of health to capacity building from the previous emphasis on disease prevention. As such, capacity building recognizes that many determinants of health reside outside the health sector. Public health officials not only have an obligation to ensure the well-being of others; they also have policing power to compel individuals with health issues to do particular things in order to ensure security of the collectivity. Because the emphasis is on improving the health of populations, public health officials continually face ethical conundrums with respect to balancing individual liberties with the rights of the groups.

While sharing information for the purpose of medical research, health promotion, and containment of disease is clearly beneficial for society, history has taught us that these goals can be displaced by those that are far less benign, such as genetic discrimination based on faulty science. The balancing act that state authorities must perform is further complicated by an increasingly globalized world where diseases are not contained within national boundaries. As such, states must work with other states to determine what information must be shared and what must be protected. Global threats to health may in fact be the most significant transboundary issue that contributes to the growth of global governance.

MANAGING HEALTH INFORMATION

Of all the information that is collected from individuals, medical information is considered by many to be the most sensitive. This information not only provides clues to our genetic makeup but also gives insights into our physical vulnerabilities and lifestyle choices that impact our health. This same information is extremely useful to researchers in determining the causes of disease and other threats to health. The balance between the autonomy of the individual and, in particular, an individual's right to privacy must be weighed against the good derived from society through the sharing of this information.

It was argued earlier that the balance struck between access and privacy is both culturally specific and epoch-sensitive. Nowhere is this more obvious than in the management of health information. Actions that the Western world now considers travesties of justice with respect to the right to autonomy of particular populations were thought, less than half a century ago, to be based on scientifically informed assumptions. Ideas regarding the inherent inferiority of certain groups of people are still used in an effort to justify discrimination.[20] It is for this reason that the ethical use of medical information has become its own sector of academic inquiry. Similarly, the advent of new technologies that allow the dissemination of information quickly and easily has raised many questions about the electronic management of health information. Yet these new technologies that provide easy access to information provide huge efficiencies both in terms of financial costs and patient treatment. For the custodians of medical information, these are relatively new questions for which there are no easy answers. The ways in which technology can benefit society appear at times to be limitless, but so too do the threats. The next chapter examines new technological innovations in surveillance that, like the electronic health record, provide certain advantages but also have a darker side.

CH_5
*Surveillance in
the Digital Age*

SURVEILLANCE AS A FORM OF SOCIAL CONTROL

Surveillance has become the norm in the twenty-first century, and it takes many forms. Cameras record individuals making purchases at a liquor store and walking through a public park; an onboard Global Positioning System (GPS) receiver tells parents where their teenager has taken their car; software gathers information that people post to social networking sites for perusal by their employer; tape recordings are made "for quality assurance" when customers phone their insurance company; and tags embedded in products allow companies and consumers to track the movement of shipped items. These technologies are used to increase efficiency, security, and accountability in all sectors. At first blush it would seem that the privacy concern with surveillance relates to individual privacy interests. But as demonstrated in chapter 1, transparency can flow in many directions. Large organizations can use surveillance techniques to monitor the activities of individuals; however, it is possible to turn the tools of surveillance on the organization in order to ensure its accountability to customers or citizens. Issues surrounding surveillance thus manifest a familiar pattern, one that is explored in this book. In and of itself, surveillance is not necessarily a bad thing; the challenge is to determine the appropriate balance between the promotion of accessibility and the curtailment of the privacy of those from whom information is collected.

Like privacy, surveillance is not a new concept: it has been the subject of attention from political philosophers and science fiction writers alike. In the eighteenth century, the political philosopher Jeremy Bentham developed the idea of the "panopticon," a proposal for the design of efficient prisons as an alternative to transporting felons to penal colonies like Australia. The design of these prisons allowed a single guard to keep multiple prisoners separated from one another and under twenty-four-hour surveillance while he himself remained unseen. Although a particular prisoner would not actually be observed by the guard all the time, the idea that he might be under surveillance would serve as a powerful constraint on the prisoner's behaviour. Though Bentham's design is often invoked as one of the earliest models of social control that curtails privacy through surveillance, Bentham addresses accountability through its emphasis on transparency. With Bentham's model, those doing the watching are themselves watched. He says:

> I take for granted as a matter of course, that under the necessary regulations for preventing interruption and disturbance, the doors of these establishments will be,

as, without very special reasons to the contrary, the doors of all public establishments ought to be, thrown wide open to the body of the curious at large — the great *open committee* of the tribunal of the world. And who ever objects to such publicity, where it is practicable, but those whose motives for objection afford the strongest reasons for it?[1] (Emphasis in the original.)

Just as the prisoner is constrained by the possibility of being watched, so too is the guard; at any time someone might drop in unexpectedly and observe his daily routine.

Writing two centuries later, the French philosopher, sociologist, and historian Michel Foucault used Bentham's concept of the panopticon as a metaphor to describe forms of scrutiny that developed in the wake of reforms intended to eliminate the brutal physical punishment of prisoners and that have come to characterize late-twentieth-century societies. In *Discipline and Punish: The Birth of the Prison*, Foucault argued that the modern, gentler form of disciplinary power, that of "normalization," or the expectation that people will achieve a particular standard, is a far more pervasive and effective method of eradicating social deviance and forcing social conformity. From a Foucauldian perspective, knowledge and power are intertwined, as knowledge is critical for the exercise of power, and power is critical for knowing. The few who control the standards effectively control the many. In contrast, sociologist Thomas Mathiesen reverses the principle of the panopticon — the single agent who watches multiple people. As he points out, the advent of TV and other forms of mass communication has resulted in surveillance by the many of the few. As such, the self-control that allows individuals to fit into modern capitalist society can happen through the reverse of the panopticon: the synopticon.[2]

These insights give pause to privacy advocates who recognize the enormous potential for the exercise of power by those entities and individuals who are in a position to collect information. Like transparency, the object of surveillance can be inward, outward, upward, or downward. If knowledge is indeed synonymous with power, surveillance has the potential to concentrate power in the hands of the few, or distribute it into the hands of the many. As the next section demonstrates, new technologies are creating increasingly powerful tools for surveillance. These same technologies, however, are blurring the lines between the watchers and the watched. As such, surveillance can be both a tool for social control and a tool for enhancing accountability.

MODERN FORMS OF WATCHING

The theme of an all-knowing, all-controlling surveillance state was popularized by the British writer George Orwell in his book *Nineteen Eighty-Four*. Written during the immediate postwar period, Orwell's novel painted a bleak picture of a dystopia in the year 1984 wherein "Big Brother" kept constant watch over citizens, monitoring and controlling every aspect of their lives. Fast forward a little more than twenty years from the year in the book's title to a report prepared for the Information Commissioner of the United Kingdom that begins with the statement: "We live in a surveillance society." The opening of the report conjures up Foucault's panopticon with its observation that "the surveillance society is better thought of as the outcome of modern organizational practices, businesses, government and the military than as a covert conspiracy."[3] Whether it is done by design or by accident, the modern "surveillance society" represents a fundamental departure from the types of societies that existed in the past.

According to the report prepared for the Information Commissioner, surveillance can be thought of as a set of activities that share certain characteristics:

> Where we find purposeful, routine, systematic and focused attention paid to personal details, for the sake of control, entitlement, management, influence or protection, we are looking at surveillance.
>
> To break this down:
>
> - The attention is first *purposeful*; the watching has a point that can be justified, in terms of control, entitlement, or some other publicly agreed goal.
>
> - Then it is *routine*; it happens as we all go about our daily business, it's in the weave of life.
>
> - But surveillance is also *systematic*; it is planned and carried out according to a schedule that is rational, not merely random.
>
> - Lastly, it is *focused*; surveillance gets down to details. While some surveillance depends on aggregate data, much refers to identifiable persons, whose data are collected, stored, transmitted, retrieved, compared, mined and traded.[4] (Emphasis in the original.)

What this means is that walking through a tourist area videotaping your surroundings with your Handycam video recorder is not considered surveillance because it is a one-off event that records randomly selected things for your own pleasure. In contrast, a camera installed at a strategic spot along that same street to film the patrons who routinely come out of a local bar intoxicated and proceed to urinate on the street or vandalize local businesses is purposeful (identifying wrongdoers), routine, systematic, and focused. Similarly, a proud parent videotaping his child playing with her nanny in a park on a sunny Sunday afternoon would not fit the definition of surveillance. Installing a camera at a daycare to enable parents to view the interaction of their children with their caregivers on demand would be considered surveillance. Many parents insert the so-called "nanny cams" surreptitiously in items like teddy bears to ensure that their children are taken care of in a manner that they find appropriate. Instances of abuse caught by this surveillance have been posted to the Internet, creating predictable rage among those viewing the videos — an example of how panopticon surveillance can become synopticon surveillance. While the latter brings with it its own set of problems, it gives hope to those who fear that surveillance will result in the top-down surveillance described by George Orwell.

Video Cameras
Thus far, a large component of the surveillance debate has revolved around the use of video cameras. This is not surprising given that video technology is one of the oldest tools of surveillance; portable versions of these cameras have been in use since the 1970s. Cameras are used for a variety

of purposes, but with respect to surveillance, they have primarily been used to enhance security. While surveillance of a child and a caregiver might result in evidence of wrongdoing that would lead to criminal charges, or at the very least reprimands or termination of employment, the utility of surveillance cameras in public places is far less clear. Some uses of cameras are not particularly contentious; they provide a clear benefit for those who may at some point themselves be filmed. Motor vehicle associations use cameras to give drivers fixed-interval camera shots of highways so they can see for themselves what road conditions and visibility are like. Skiers can check the conditions of ski slopes by looking at images of the hill. The most popular reason to use cameras in public places, however, is for law enforcement purposes. Cameras are used in lobbies of buildings that restrict access so that occupants can see who is requesting entry into the building. They are also used in stores and banks to catch thieves. Schools use them to detect people in the school who should not be there and to monitor the behaviour of students. Such examples often concern places that are public in the sense that anyone can go into them but private in the sense that they are located on privately owned property. For the most part, these uses generate limited controversy; a citizen who does not want to be caught on camera can choose to patronize a different establishment.

It is the cameras installed in purely public places for crime prevention purposes that are particularly controversial. Police use photo radar to ticket speeders and red light violators on public roadways. Cameras are also used in municipal parks, in plazas, and on sidewalks. These are all public spaces that everyone has access to. With respect to photo radar, drivers who are not breaking the law do not have to worry about their image being captured on camera. But law-abiding citizens walking through a public park or plaza have the same likelihood of having their images captured as criminals who pass through the same space. This has resulted in a debate over whether the law enforcement value of videotaping citizens is worth giving up the right to enjoy that space without privacy being compromised.

Those who support video surveillance claim that cameras that are routinely monitored have a positive effect on public safety because they serve as suspicious activity detectors that can alert law enforcement authorities to the possibility that a crime is about to be committed. Obviously, sending police officers to the scene earlier rather than later will put them in a better position to apprehend criminals. Moreover, it is argued that if criminals are aware that they are being watched via a camera, they are less likely to commit a crime. For this reason, most cameras are highly visible to the public so that there is no doubt for perpetrators that they are being watched. If a crime is committed, investigators are able to use the collected images to assist in their investigation and as evidence in their prosecution of a crime.

Critics of video surveillance as a useful tool in law enforcement point out, however, that most cameras are not monitored in "real time." That is, no one is watching the camera as the crime is committed; rather, the videotape will be reviewed "after the fact" to assist in the investigation and prosecution of a crime. Critics claim that crime prevention is a misnomer in the case of video surveillance; crime displacement is more accurate. Accordingly, criminals will simply shift the site of their activities from the area under surveillance to one where there are no cameras. The net effect on crime reduction will thus be minimal.

In 2005, the British Home Office produced a comprehensive report assessing the impact of closed-circuit television (CCTV) cameras. The report included a review of existing research that painted a mixed picture of the effectiveness of CCTVs in reducing crime. On the one hand, CCTVs appear to have little impact on impulsive crimes (such as those related to alcohol) or on personal crime (such as assault). On the other hand, CCTVs do appear to reduce crimes related to property, and in particular to vehicles, especially those in parking lots. That said, even those who found a reduction in crime related to vehicles speculated that other factors might be coming into play. Crime displacement did occur, although it was not found to be that common and was more evident in relation to some crimes than others. Offenders did not seem particularly concerned with the possibility that CCTVs could be used to convict them of crimes, although offenders who had been convicted through CCTV evidence felt significantly more threatened by their presence.[5] As the report notes, however, the difficulty with these studies is that they do not try to address the issue of effectiveness. In particular, the cost-effectiveness of installing CCTVs for the purpose of reducing crime "has been largely ignored."[6]

Perhaps the most damning criticism of video surveillance for crime reduction is the concern that the captured images will be used for purposes other than those they were originally collected for. This phenomenon is referred to as "function creep."[7] Examples of function creep typically revolve around the use of personal data for advertising, marketing research, or identifying trends. This is of particular concern where the line between the public and the private becomes blurred and the public purpose of collecting information becomes mixed with the commercial purpose of using information for targeted advertising. But function creep can also refer to voyeurism, commercial entertainment, and blackmail. While most jurisdictions have clear laws with respect to the collection of personal information in the form of wiretaps for voice, legislation regarding the collection, use, and retention of visual images of citizens is far less developed. Clearly, the objectives of installing surveillance cameras must be unambiguously outlined. How these objectives are defined and by whom should be equally clear. Security firms have a vested interest in the installation of their cameras in public spaces. If the firm not only provides the cameras but is also contracted by government to operate them, this raises the troubling issue of the privatization of public spaces by businesses that might not have the same agenda as a public organization. Moreover, businesses that are contracted to provide public services are not subjected to the same level of control as their public sector equivalents.[8]

Civil libertarians are particularly vociferous opponents of video surveillance. They bemoan the limitations it places on citizens' rights to move about and conduct their daily business without having their privacy rights infringed. In particular, they note that surveillance has a chilling effect on freedom of assembly and movement. As Nigel Waters argues: "Most people have an instinctive aversion to being watched. The chilling effect of surveillance is difficult to quantify, but is clearly recognised by the public."[9] Cameras can be used as an instrument of social control, monitoring the activities of those the state has deemed to be anti-social or non-conforming, even if their behaviour does not break the law. Equity issues are raised, as the rich are less likely than the poor and the marginalized to frequent public spaces that are under surveillance. Others raise the spectre of minorities being targeted by racial profiling. As Tator and Henry observe:

> When we examine the histories of people of African descent in Western nations, we find that these forms of social control include intense surveillance by law enforcement authorities resulting in increased rates of interaction between police and people of African descent. These interactions have contributed to higher-than-average rates of arrests, convictions, incarcerations, and acts of violence and have resulted in physical harm and death.[10]

In Canada, the same observation can be made about those of Aboriginal descent and, in Europe, about those of Roma descent (that is, the gypsies). Since the terrorist attacks in the United States in 2001, those who are or appear to be Middle Eastern are apt to experience more intense screening than other passengers when they pass through airport security. While it can be argued that elevated crime rates in a particular community correlate with a higher incidence of involvement in illegal activities, it is also true that more criminal activity will be detected in a particular group if proportionally more people in that group are questioned.

The dizzying speed of technological innovation has increased the significance of the observation that we live in a surveillance society. The number of new technologies coming on stream daily suggests that we can expect more surveillance in the future rather than less. As such, the utility and purpose of surveillance techniques must be scrutinized. This is particularly true given that the combination of video monitoring with new communications media opens up new and even more powerful forms of surveillance; this is the focus of the next section.

The Internet

Until a few years ago, the Internet was used primarily for peer-to-peer email communication. The advent of YouTube and social networking sites, however, represents a profound change with respect to how people communicate. Whereas a video camera used to be mainly the tool of choice of the proud parents capturing the first steps of their toddler, a huge range of people now routinely use this technology due to the combination of the increasingly portable and easy-to-use video technology with the ability to broadcast to millions quickly and cheaply. The dissemination of video clips is done for political, commercial, social, and religious purposes, but it is the marriage of video and Internet technologies that takes surveillance to new levels. This is illustrated by two commercial uses of recorded images: Internet Eyes and Google Street View.

In an attempt to make better use of the data being collected by CCTV cameras, a savvy entrepreneur launched "Internet Eyes." This Internet game allows players to plug into Britain's CCTV network in order to scour images for the purpose of detecting and reporting people committing crimes. Those who report the most crimes can win monthly prizes of up to one thousand pounds. The website contains a rogues' gallery of suspected criminals, their offences, and the name of the player who caught them. While some business owners embrace the idea of posting a sign that says "Internet Eyes Patrol Here," civil liberties groups denounce the initiative as a "snooper's paradise" that would result in the most minor of misdemeanours being broadcast to the world. Others liken the constant watching and reporting to situations in former communist states or even Orwell's *Nineteen Eighty-Four*, wherein families, neighbours, and friends would denounce one another to the authorities.

By April 2010, the site had attracted 14,659 registered gamers and the attention of the non-profit privacy advocacy groups No CCTV and Privacy International. As a result of the many questions they raised regarding the verification of who was watching and the possibility for surreptitious retention of images from the site by third parties, the company delayed the launch of this synopticon form of surveillance until Internet Eyes addressed privacy concerns raised by the UK Information Commissioner's office.[11] In October 2010, the commissioner's office gave Internet Eyes permission to launch for a three-month trial period, a decision that received condemnation from No CCTV and Privacy International. In a joint press release, Charles Farrier of No CCTV said:

> The Information Commissioner has put private profit above personal privacy in allowing a private company to launch its Stasi style citizen spy game rather than defending the rights of British citizens. This is the privatisation of the surveillance society — a private company asking private individuals to spy on each other using private cameras connected to the Internet. Internet Eyes must be challenged.[12]

In January 2011, Internet Eyes announced a Canadian partnership and the launch of the game in Dartmouth, Nova Scotia.

Another synopticon form of surveillance, Google Street View, has garnered attention from privacy advocates who claim it is unacceptably privacy-invasive. Google Street View, launched in 2007, is an enhanced version of Google Maps, a web-based mapping service that uses Global Positioning System (GPS) technology to allow users to locate particular addresses. The addition of Street View allows users to actually see pictures of the houses and buildings associated with the address they type in. The service, which offers 360° horizontal and 290° vertical panoramic street views, is provided through the use of cameras perched on top of a car at a height of two and a half metres. The images recorded by the cameras are then assembled to create a 360° view and matched to a particular location using GPS devices.[13]

Although people such as tourism officials and real estate agents might find this technology helpful, privacy advocates do not. The trouble is that people and items such as licence plates that can be linked to specific people are sometimes caught in the photographs. Moreover, although the cameras are located in public space (the street), they are high enough that they can capture images of people on their private property (in their fenced backyard, for instance). A woman hiding from an abusive spouse or a couple entering an abortion clinic are just a few examples of people who might object to their images being available on Google Street View. Websites such as StreetViewFun have already popped up where "interesting" photos are posted — women sunbathing, men and women with hands over their groins or breasts "adjusting" their underwear, a woman bending over so that her thong and buttocks are exposed, men urinating at the side of the road, men walking into adult book stores and sex shops, and a man passed out drunk on the side of the road.[14] Individuals can request to have images of themselves removed, but the image may already have been downloaded before it is removed from Street View, at which point Google no longer controls the image.

In response to privacy commissioners around the world expressing concern over this form of synopticon, as of May 2008 Google began blurring the faces of people and images of licence plates. Google announced in 2010, however, that its European service might be suspended because the privacy-related requirements of the European Union make the costs of the service prohibitive.[15] Google Street View ran into even more trouble that same year when it was discovered that the cameras on top of its cars had been gathering data from unencrypted home WiFi networks for three years. Google called the data collection an accident and blamed the security gaffe on old code. Others, like Stephen Conroy, Australia's Minister for Broadband, Communications and the Digital Economy, are less generous. Google's CEO Eric Schmidt has strongly criticized Conroy in the past for his plan to implement an Internet filter for Australia that would block certain websites (such as ones featuring child pornography). Conroy hit back by claiming that the Google data collection might be "the largest privacy breach in history across Western democracies," and that it is "a bit creepy."[16] But for those who are concerned with personal autonomy, whether it is the government censoring what is on the Internet or Google undertaking surveillance, individual freedom is being curtailed.

What is particularly interesting about the so-called

"Google WiSpy" controversy is the cultural differences among countries when it comes to surveillance and privacy. Once issues are raised, however, cultural convergence is evident, as countries tend to adopt similar views of privacy events. Google Street View was launched in the United States with barely a whisper of opposition. The privacy commissioner in Canada voiced concerns about images that had previously been collected in the US, and in response, Google notified Canadians when it began filming for Street View. Contrast this to Google's response to much stronger criticism in Japan. To address the Japanese unease that Street View cameras were able to look over fences into private residences, Google reshot all its images with cameras that had been lowered by 40 centimetres. In Greece, the Data Protection Agency banned Google from collecting photos until the company addressed storage, retention, and consent concerns.[17] Despite the already pervasive surveillance by CCTV cameras in Britain, villagers in the town of Broughton surrounded a Google camera car and refused to let it come into their town. In Switzerland, the country's privacy watchdog asked Google to remove pictures of fenced yards and private streets, to blur the faces of people and images of licence plates, and to notify jurisdictions one week in advance of filming. Eventually, it took Google to federal court because "Google for the most part declined to comply with the requests."[18] Germany and the Czech Republic launched investigations into the WiSpy matter.

While different countries initially had different reactions to Google's filming, issues that were raised in one jurisdiction have had a domino effect. Concern came full circle in the US on 26 May 2010, when the group Consumer Watchdog wrote the attorneys general of the states and territories and requested that they launch their own investigations. In its letter, the group charged that:

> Google's claim that its intrusive behavior was by "mistake" stretches all credulity. In fact, Google has demonstrated a history of pushing the envelope and then apologizing when its overreach is discovered. Given its recent record of privacy abuses, there is absolutely no reason to trust anything the Internet giant claims about its data collection policies.[19]

Undoubtedly the initial reaction to Google Street View's activities would be different yet again if Google had started filming in China, India, Iran, or Brazil rather than North America, Europe, and Australia. Ironically, the very technology that allows easy access to images worldwide with a click of the mouse that many find so objectionable is also the technology that enables the circulation of privacy concerns worldwide. Attitudes toward privacy vary across countries, but there is also considerable convergence that results from the dissemination of concern and the subsequent globalized debate.

The combination of video and the Internet is a powerful tool for information dissemination. What is of concern is when "communication" is harnessed for the overt goal of surveillance (as in the case of Internet Eyes), or when surveillance is a by-product of the new innovation (as in the case of Google Street View). The Internet, however, can be combined with other technologies that have far greater implications for the development of the "surveillance society." The example of radio-frequency identification tracking devices is the subject of the next section.

Radio-Frequency Identification Tracking Devices

The radio-frequency identification device (RFID) is a tracking system that can be embedded in objects. These systems can improve the efficiency of production and service processes, but they are controversial because they comprise a "hidden" system of surveillance. RFID systems consist of a transponder, a reader, and a back office system. A transponder, commonly known as an RFID tag, transmits data by emitting radio waves. This information is collected by readers, which can be mobile, such as a barcode scanner, or fixed at certain locations, such as a vehicle toll gateway. Data collected by a reader are sent to a back office or a data processing system.[20] RFID tags may be passive or active. Passive tags must be in the range of a reader in order to operate because they lack an internal power source. Active tags have an internal power source that allows them to emit radio waves. Active tags have a much greater "read range" than passive tags, and in some cases, can be read up to several kilometres away. As well, active tags have more memory and better processing than passive ones.[21] An active tag, then, enables the data processing system to keep tabs on an item that is in movement. While tracking an object is is an innocuous goal, it is the tracking of the person in possession of the object that causes concern; this constitutes a sophisticated form of surveillance.

RFID tags are embedded in a growing number of personal items and identity documents such as employee and student identification cards, library books, tire pressure monitoring, parking permits, luggage in airports, mail, livestock, residential garbage pay-for-what you-dispose bins, and bracelets worn by prison inmates or guards.[22] The concern over surveillance notwithstanding, RFID technology can benefit individuals in the areas of safety, convenience, and accessibility. RFID tags in enhanced driver's licences transmit a unique code to a reader containing such personal information as nationality. An anticipated benefit of this use is the reduction in lineups at border crossings between the US and Canada. RFIDs also can be used to trace food, shorten supermarket queues, and track patients suffering from Alzheimer's disease.

The consumer benefits from RFIDs are endless. RFID technology is being used in the development of the successor to the bar code, the Electronic Producer Code (EPC). EPCs identify each individual item that is manufactured using RFID tags, as opposed to identifying just the class of product and the manufacturer. A university student in Lethbridge, Alberta, who has purchased a computer online can now track the movement of her new computer using her old computer: from the factory that produced it in China, to the North American point of entry in Alaska, to the UPS distribution centre in Kentucky, to the American point of exit, Buffalo, to the Canadian USB distribution centre in Winnipeg, to the western Canada air hub in Calgary, and then finally, to the student's home in Lethbridge. For the producer of the computer, the RFID tag can track the product from the point of manufacture to the point of sale, reducing inventory, labour costs, and stock losses. Anyone who has experienced the frustration of losing a wallet or a cellphone can immediately see the benefits of tagging personal possessions that can be easily mislaid. A recent report of the Australian Law Reform Commission concluded that RFIDs can be used to "benefit individuals, businesses and government."[23]

Critics of RFID technology point out that tags incorporate little security, transmitting signals to authorized and unauthorized users alike, enabling hackers to "skim" data from them. Moreover, ignorance of the RFID tagging of an item leaves people wearing or carrying them vulnerable to surreptitious surveillance. The trade-off between privacy and security in an RFID tag embedded in a teddy bear carried by a two-year-old in a daycare might seem reasonable. But what about the RFID-tagged cellphone that is carried by an eighteen-year-old high school student? Parents now have the ability to track their children's every move, even if that child is legally an adult. RFIDs also give jealous spouses the ability to track their partners' whereabouts and an employer the ability to determine if an employee driving a delivery truck has made an unscheduled stop to pick up dry cleaning and a takeout coffee on company time. And what about RFIDs embedded in products that the consumer buys that give unknown people the ability to track the movements of the person who purchased the product?

To date, the response to these security concerns has seen the development of voluntary codes as opposed to government regulation. EPCglobal Incorporated identifies four principles as fundamental in governing the use of RFID tags in consumer goods: consumers should be given clear notice of the use of EPC on the products or the packaging; the choices available to remove or disable EPC tags on products should be readily available; accurate information about both EPC and its applications should be provided; and no personally identifiable information should be contained, collected, or stored by the EPC.[24] The purpose of these guidelines is to increase consumer confidence in RFID tags by anticipating and dealing with privacy concerns as they arise. While RFID technology benefits both consumers and producers, it does present challenges for privacy protection by dramatically changing the privacy landscape. With that, RFID also has the potential to dramatically change social norms around privacy. Specifically, surveillance by "Big Brother" that a few decades ago would have been seen as so invasive as to be socially unacceptable might become the norm for those who are being watched. This is particularly true for young people who have grown accustomed to being tracked by their parents and filmed by video cameras at school.

Those concerned with the increasing use of surveillance technologies lament that innovations such as Internet Eyes, Google Street View, and RFIDs take us down a path of social control that we should avoid at all costs. The events of 11 September 2001 elevated the issue of security by heightening the sense of vulnerability of the Western world to terrorism. This insecurity has spawned a multi-billion dollar industry, referred to as the global security-industrial complex.[25] Security is linked tightly with surveillance and is of particular concern in relation to "mega-events" such as global political summits or sporting events such as the Olympics. When public fear of terrorism and crime is harnessed to support the new technologies to fight them, the concern for personal autonomy is considerably diminished.

Securing Mega-Events

The Olympic Games are a particularly interesting example of a mega-event where security trumps all. No global event captures the imagination (and the attention) of the global public like the Olympic Games. The eyes of the world are on the host city for the duration of the games, with spectators enthusiastically cheering on their national teams and applauding the feats of the world's most talented athletes. But the games are far more than a sporting event — they provide a massive advertising platform both for corporations and social activists, who use them to sell products and promote social causes. The former activity, that of marketing products, is accepted as a critical component of athletic sponsorship, so much so that the power of the state is harnessed to protect the property rights of corporations with respect to the use of logos or brands that are associated with the Olympics. The platform for social activism, however, is less enthusiastically embraced. Indeed, the power of the state is used to monitor the activities of those who might use the opportunity of the mega-event to advance a particular social cause. That said, even the activists' detractors grudgingly acknowledge that the ability to protest is a hallmark of a free and democratic society, and as such, the protesters must be tolerated. What is far more troubling is the prospect of protestors resorting to violent acts to draw attention to their cause. This concern is the unfortunate legacy of the 1972 Munich Olympic Games, where terrorists killed eleven Israeli athletes. Twenty years later two people were killed and 111 were injured from the detonation of a pipe bomb at Centennial Olympic Park during the Atlanta Olympics. Providing athletes, officials, and the general public with sufficient security to enjoy the games without fear of becoming a victim of a politically inspired act of violence has become a major preoccupation of Olympic organizers. The recent Winter Olympics in Vancouver is a case in point: the security budget for those games was close to a billion dollars.[26] Similarly, the combined price tag for two other mega-events, the G8 and the G20 global summits held in Ontario in June 2010, was about the same amount.[27]

What is troubling for those concerned about privacy protection is the "security function creep" that happens as a result of hosting an Olympic event. Security contractors and police use the mega-event to introduce a technological solution for a particular security issue. While the proposed solution might not initially be considered palatable as routine security, after its use at an event it becomes far easier to employ it in more ordinary venues. The trajectory happens something like this. New technologies are devised to address the specific security needs of an Olympic Games. The public tends to be much more tolerant of new and more invasive security protection measures because they are introduced during the one-off Olympic event. The new technologies then become the standard for future games. The media coverage of the security measures serves to normalize security practices that might otherwise be deemed too privacy-invasive to be acceptable. The security contractors capitalize on the prestige they gain from their role in keeping the games safe, which enhances their credibility when they introduce new technologies in the future. As a report on security and the Vancouver Olympics put it: "Designed for the unique risks of an exceptional global sporting event and driven by the search for new markets and profits, the technologies, expertise and contracts characteristic of Olympic security therefore risk dispersing into more mundane contexts, simultaneously routinizing and intensifying security."[28] Thus, one of the legacies of mega-events is usually increased surveillance. Given the immense amount of money to be made from marketing surveillance technologies, this legacy can hardly be seen as an unintended outcome of mega-events but rather an outcome that was leveraged from the opportunity the events provided.

An example of a mega-event that resulted in obvious function creep is the National Football League Super Bowl game in Tampa Florida in 2001. Every spectator's facial image was scanned and compared to a data bank of known terrorists using a combination of cameras and biometric technology. After the event, the cameras were deployed to a Tampa neighbourhood; streets and public spaces were monitored. This was done without even informing the residents, much less asking their consent.[29] This type of function creep frequently happens in localities that host Olympic events, as is evidenced by the debate about what will happen with the cameras that were installed for use at the Vancouver Olympics. Although Vancouverites have resisted the installation of surveillance cameras in public places in the past, thousands of cameras were installed in the weeks preceding to the games. The billion-dollar question now is whether all these cameras will be removed or whether some will continue to be used post-Olympics for the purposes of routine law enforcement.

Surveillance cameras in public spaces may become more appealing to Vancouverites as a result of the city's hosting the 2011 Stanley Cup hockey playoffs. The final game saw the convergence of an estimated one hundred thousand fans in downtown Vancouver to watch the game on a specially installed giant-screen TV. After the Vancouver team lost, a riot broke out. Despite the efforts of police, who used tear gas in an effort to contain the riot, the mob caused millions of dollars of damage to public property, businesses, and parked cars. Rioters brazenly took pictures and videos of themselves vandalizing and looting property and posted them to Facebook and YouTube. Afterward, the province's vehicle insurance company, ICBC, provided police with its database of driver's license pictures so that the police could use face recognition software to identify individuals who appeared in crowd photographs. Facebook pages sprang up asking people to post photos they'd taken on cellphones so that rioters could be identified. Names, addresses, and phone numbers were subsequently shared online, as a result of which some of the accused chose to leave their homes for fear of retribution from outraged Vancouverites who were not involved in the destruction. This incident provides yet another example of function creep (a photo taken for licensing purposes is used to determine that a citizen participated in a riot), but it also constitutes an interesting manifestation of synopticon surveillance along the lines of the Internet Eyes game discussed earlier in this chapter.[30]

In other venues, the installation of cameras is already a fait accompli. Britain has the distinction of having the most CCTV cameras per capita of any nation in the world, with estimates ranging from 1.2 to 4.2 million CCTVs nationwide.[31] While surveillance might increase people's perception that the streets are safer, there are no strong indications that cameras significantly reduce crime. This is in part due to the poor quality of the images and the sheer volume of them. Detective Chief Inspector Mick Neville of the London police observes that only 3 percent of London's street robberies are solved as a result of video surveillance. Given the billions of pounds spent on installing the cameras, Neville's assessment of the CCTV initiative is that "it's been an utter fiasco."[32] Despite these criticisms of CCTV use and the lack of evidence supporting their effectiveness, there appears to be little political appetite for removing them from public spaces in Britain or elsewhere.

As will be illustrated in the next section, surveillance (like transparency) can operate in different directions. It is certainly true that those in positions of authority can use surveillance to exert social control over their subordinates. It is equally true, however, that the combination of surveillance with Internet technologies has the potential to force accountability on those in authority. This trend began with the proliferation of cheap, portable video cameras and has accelerated with the widespread use of the Internet as a source of social and political information.

Watching the Workers and Watching the Watchers
Surveillance as a method of increasing the productivity of workers builds naturally on the work of management theorists who subscribe to the "command and control" school of thought. This perspective is grounded in Frederick Taylor's *The Principles of Scientific Management* (1967), which separates decision making from work and workers from management. Taylor saw workers as poorly educated, lazy, and uninterested in organizational goals. Their goal was to receive the maximum pay for minimal effort. Given these assumptions, managers devised various strategies to "keep workers honest" and to improve productivity. Many of these strategies involved overt surveillance. In the past, this would have consisted of a supervisor walking around the factory floor watching employees work. Today, this surveillance might be carried out with the help of video cameras. But the video camera is not the only tool by which individuals can be watched. A software program called Social Sentry allows employers to monitor employees' social networking activities on such sites as Facebook and Twitter. This is a much more sophisticated

version of previous technology that counted an employee's keystrokes on a computer or a cash register, as Social Sentry monitors the employees' social networking activities on any device or network, including mobile ones. Employers can now easily track posts made by an employee that are indiscreet, spill trade secrets, suggest corporate wrongdoing, or are otherwise perceived to be counter to the employer's interests.[33]

A somewhat more covert method of surveillance is the tracking of data that can be used to identify a specific individual — a practice that Roger Clarke has called "dataveillance": the automated monitoring of people's activities or communications through the use of information technologies.[34] Biometric technology relies on attributes that are unique to a particular individual, such as a fingerprint, retinal patterns, or voice. Biometrics have been used by companies to identify customers who phone in to make changes to their accounts, to provide employees with access to buildings, or to record their time of arrival at the job site via an electronically activated time clock. This technology is also popular in the realm of public security. Travellers passing through London's Heathrow airport, for example, must routinely submit to a retinal scan. Travellers have, however, objected far less to the recording and storage of this form of personal information than they have to American "enhanced security" measures that entail asking airline customers to submit to full body scanning by means of backscatter X-ray machines. These machines produce images of travellers' naked bodies, a procedure that clearly strikes airline customers as more invasive of personal privacy. Although security officials claim that these images are not retained, evidence to the contrary has emerged.[35]

The international corporate grocer Whole Foods took data-veillance to a new level when it announced an additional "healthy member" staff discount for those employees whose biometric criteria met certain standards — employees "who are willing to undergo surveillance of a selection of body measures (blood pressure, cholesterol tests, and BMI calculations) and refrain from nicotine use." [36] Whole Foods says the purpose of the program is to promote healthy lifestyle choices that will result in the reduction of health plan costs. The collection of biometric data for the purpose of improving the bottom line of a business is troubling for privacy advocates, however, as is the storage and monitoring of health information by an employer and the sense of ownership over employees' personal autonomy that the company gains through this form of physical surveillance.

While surveillance in the workplace is used to increase productivity and efficiency, its benefits remain unclear. The debate between those who feel that accountability (and thus productivity) can be improved through the development of top-down external controls and those who favour fostering internal control based on individual restraint is an old one that will not be resolved here. [37] A modern twist to this debate, however, is that the tools of surveillance can be reversed so that the watchers become the watched.

Pessimists despair that the power of large multinational companies and nations such as the United States is unassailable; they are convinced that privacy is dead and that the conglomeration of power within large all-knowing and all-seeing entities is inevitable. But new technology can be used to reverse the direction of transparency; it allows the activities of those in authority to be easily disseminated, thus pointing the synopticon gaze in the opposite direction. Moreover, email, social networking, cellphones, and Twitter enable the mobilization and circulation of dissenters who can be everywhere and nowhere at the same, making them a difficult target for those who want to silence them. The so-called "Handycam revolution" began with a video shot in 1991. From the balcony of his apartment building, George Holliday videotaped white Los Angeles police officers beating a black man, Rodney King. Holliday gave the video to a local TV station. The video caused outrage and immediate action against the offending officers; it demonstrated the power of the individual with a recorder vis-à-vis large institutions. Everyone with a camera-equipped cellphone in his pocket now can join the ranks of those fighting hegemonic power.

The world's most famous whistle-blower is currently Julian Assange, a former hacker who has committed himself to "radical transparency." He is the mastermind behind the Sunshine Press, an organization that brings together civil liberty activists and computer experts to run the website WikiLeaks.com. The organization posts all kinds of documents: from diplomatic cables, protocols from Guantánamo Bay, celebrity tax returns, emails from Sarah Palin's personal account, exposés of toxic dumping in Africa, and 9/11 pager messages. Documents are delivered to a digital dead drop — in this case a Swedish computer server that is protected by that country's strong whistle-blowers' protection laws. Once the data are received, WikiLeaks puts out a call on Twitter for assistance in de-encrypting classified documents. Once de-encryption is accomplished, it posts the declassified documents on its website. Because WikiLeaks.com uses servers located in various countries, the court-ordered shutdown of its US server in 2008 over the disclosure of the activities of a Swiss bank had little effect on the organization's activities. It now boasts the posting of over a million documents. As the presiding judge in the American case noted: "We live in an age when people can do some good things and people can do some terrible things without accountability necessarily in a court of law."[38]

WikiLeaks gained notoriety when it posted "Collateral Murder" on its website on 5 April 2010.[39] This US military video shows the graphic killing of a dozen men and the wounding of two children on the streets of Baghdad in 2007. The video was taken from a US army Apache helicopter gunsight; the helicopter was responding to a call for help from American soldiers who had been fired upon. The clip eerily resembles a first-person shooter video game. Among the victims were a twenty-two-year-old Reuters photojournalist and his assistant. The US military showed the video to Reuters immediately after the incident; Reuters asked for an investigation and sought copies of the footage by using access to information legislation. The US investigated the incident and found no wrongdoing; the video copy was provided to Reuters two and a half years after the incident.

While some claim that the dissemination of videos of the WikiLeaks genre on YouTube is a triumph for accountability in government,[40] others argue that governments have legitimate reasons for keeping some information secret, particularly that pertaining to military engagements and national security. They fear that the power to quickly disseminate classified documents to a wide audience dramatically decreases the power of states pursuing the goals of security, democracy, and justice vis-à-vis individuals pursuing their own interests, whatever those might be. In response to the 2010 release of ninety thousand classified military documents, US National Security Adviser General James Jones asserted that this information "could put the lives of Americans and our partners at risk."[41] This debate aside, what is clear from this overview of surveillance tools and their objects is that surveillance in modern society is ubiquitous and serves a multitude of purposes. What is equally obvious is that the tools of surveillance can be focused on different objects, and as such, have the potential to create different outcomes with respect to how society functions.

WHITHER WATCHING?

At the outset of this chapter it was claimed that surveillance has become a twenty-first-century norm. It was demonstrated that surveillance brings a level of transparency to our personal and professional lives that was unimaginable even twenty years ago. When linked with the concern for security in the post–9/11 world, surveillance as a desirable societal norm becomes a formidable concept to argue against. This is particularly true with the growth of the security-industrial complex that profits handsomely from the fear of crime and terrorism that fuels the appetite for deployment of ever more sophisticated technological innovations. The increasing incidence of surveillance in all its varied forms incrementally (but steadily) chips away at our personal autonomy by decreasing our privacy.

As in other sectors, the flip side of privacy invasion is an increase in access to information. In this case, the filming of particular incidents and the circulation and dissemination of this information through television networks serve as powerful tools for accountability. The more recent ability of individuals to circulate this to even more people on the Internet through sites like YouTube or WikiLeaks totally bypasses media gatekeepers, giving every person the ability to publicly demand accountability from the government and other actors. Like transparency, surveillance can operate in different directions — it can focus on the individual or the organization. As such, it can be used as a form of social control or as a method of ensuring accountability. There can be no doubt that surveillance technology has gone a considerable distance in improving efficiencies in the production and dissemination of commercial goods. While surveillance typically is thought to concentrate power in the hands of the few, the combination of surveillance tools with mass communication devices like the Internet has potential to distribute power into the hands of the many. As has been discussed in other chapters, surveillance has implications for both information access and privacy protection. Ultimately, a balance must be struck, and this balance will reflect society's view as to the proper balance between the rights of the individual and the rights of the group.

CH_6
Social Networking:
The Case of Facebook

THE CREATION OF ONLINE PERSONALITIES

As baby boomers move from middle to old age, the defining characteristic that confirms their status as seniors surely is that they can tell the millennium generation that they remember a time when the Internet did not exist. During the boomers' coming of age during the 1960s, 1970s, and early 1980s, the global information environment revolved around sovereign states, bounded by territorial borders and often by language. With each new technological development, countries were confronted with both the desire to pursue the latest technologies associated with modernity and the need to control them in order to maintain their monopoly on authority and power. This is no less true for the Internet than it was for previous technological developments such as the printing press and the radio. The proliferation of technologies that enable information dispersal greatly enhances access to information, which, as earlier chapters argue, is critical to democratic governance. In this regard, the development of the Internet is critical to the cause of democratization of authoritarian regimes as well as the engagement of citizens in liberal democracies. As Deibert and Rohozinski observe:

> There is no doubt that the Internet has unleashed a wide-ranging and globally significant shift in communications — a shift that has led to the empowerment of individuals and nonstate actors on an unprecedented scale. . . . Just as with previous technological developments, as the Internet has grown in political significance, an architecture of control — through technology, regulation, norms, and political calculus — has emerged to shape a new geopolitical information landscape.[1]

The debate over autonomy and control of the Internet hinges on the issues of censorship (in particular with respect to pornography and social norms) and state security (terrorism and cybersecurity). Where one stands in the debate over control of the Internet reflects one's views on the proper balance between the rights of the individual versus the rights of the group within which the individual lives. As we shall see in the following, it also relates to how one perceives the proper balance between the rights of access to information versus the rights of the individual to personal privacy.

It is beyond the scope of this book to provide a discussion of the huge issue of control of the Internet. This chapter confines itself to an analysis of Facebook, a popular social networking site that has gained notoriety over its privacy practices. The issues surrounding access to information and privacy protection with respect to this particular social networking site provide a snapshot of a much larger debate. More importantly for our purposes, Facebook illustrates the huge impact that electronic information has had on our ability to both obtain information and to protect our personal autonomy.

Social network sites are a relatively recent addition to the Information Communications Technology (ICT) landscape. Boyd and Ellison define these as "web based services that allow individuals to (1) construct a public or semi-public profile within a bounded system, (2) articulate a list of other users with whom they share a connection, and (3) view and traverse their list of connections and those made by others within the system."[2] The first social networking site, Six-Degrees.com, was conceived in 1997. Building on the idea that everyone is connected to everyone else through six degrees of separation, this site allowed users to send messages and post to a bulletin board. Seven years later, students at Harvard created Facebook to encourage networking among their peers. The site quickly became a huge success, and by September 2006 the site was opened up so that anyone over the age of thirteen could join.[3]

Social networking sites such as Facebook allow the user to create an online personality through the creation of a profile that contains basic personal information such as his or her name, birthdate, current city and hometown, contact information, schools attended, employment information, interests, and political and religious views. The profile includes places to post picture albums, videos, links, favourite sayings, books, and movies. It also includes a "wall," where the user can post "status updates"— messages that range from the profound to the mundane. Users become "friends" with other users through mutual consent; friends can view each other's profiles and post messages on each other's walls. They can identify friends in their photos by "tagging" them so that when a viewer runs his cursor over the person's face, the person's name appears. Once a photo is tagged, it is posted on the friend's wall and friends of both the tagger and the tagged are alerted to its presence. Users can invite others to events or find like-minded "friends" on the Facebook network by starting up an event page or a group page. The critical point about social networking is that it allows online interaction among various people that is visible. The introduction of the "news feed" in 2006 increased this visibility when interactions (such as status updates and tagged photos) were listed in an easily scrollable page that enabled the user to track the activities of their Facebook "friends."

By 2010, the number of people using Facebook had skyrocketed, reaching half a billion users midway through the year. This achievement made Facebook the most widely used social networking site in the world. While the primary users at its inception were college students, the age of the fastest growing demographic of new users continues to increase, with some studies reporting that it is now over fifty-five. Contrary to the popular belief that young people do not care about their privacy, a study released in 2010 by the Pew Internet Organization shows exactly the opposite: young people between the ages of eighteen and twenty-nine are more concerned about and sophisticated in managing their "digital footprint" than are those thirty years old and older. This includes taking such measures as limiting the availability of their personal information online, changing privacy settings in social networking sites, deleting comments that appear on their profile, and removing their names from photos posted online. The report notes that "compared with older users, young adults are not only the most attentive to customizing their privacy settings and limiting what they share via their profiles, but they are also generally less trusting of the sites that host their content."[4]

The popularity of social networking sites is explained by the connectivity they provide — in particular, the access that they afford by allowing individuals to easily connect to others they know, or would like to know. Recent acquaintances use Facebook to get to know each other better by perusing their online profiles. For others, it has been used to reconnect with old friends. A fifty-year-old has only to type in the name of a person he attended middle school with to find his best friend from thirty-five years ago. Similarly, a student who goes to college in the town where she attended her first few years of primary school can reconnect with the little boy who befriended her on her first day of grade one. Facebook is also useful for groups: organizations or individuals can create a page for like-minded individuals to gather to promote a particular issue or cause. But the greatest impact of social networks will arguably be their impact on the creation of virtual communities. These communities take many forms; they can be social, political, or professional in nature. A characteristic of all of them is that they have changed the speed with which information can be shared and how people connect with each other to share common interests.

THE POWER AND PERILS OF VIRTUAL COMMUNITIES

Much has been written about the use of wireless technologies and the Internet for the mobilization of those with common interests. Knowledge about particular issues and events circulates easily using these new media; sharing information facilitates both social and political engagement. With information dissemination comes the dispersal of power. As explained by Manuel Castells:

> Control of information and communication has been a major source of power throughout history. The advent of the Internet and of wireless communication allows the development of many-to-many and one-to-one horizontal communication channels that bypass political or business control of communication. Therefore, new avenues are open for autonomous processes of social and political mobilization that do not rely on formal politics and do not depend on their framing in the mass media.[5]

These communications can result in a "flash mob," the seemingly spontaneous coming together of people in a public place to perform an act (such as freezing in place for a specified amount of time, dancing, singing, etc.) and then dispersing as quickly as they gathered.[6] These mobilizations have occurred in countries all over the world, including Singapore, Canada, Ukraine, Sweden, South Africa, France, Australia, Japan, and Israel. Flash mobs are organized by individuals using peer-to-peer communications technologies (such as the Internet and cellphones), effectively bypassing traditional means of communication that are slower and more likely to be centrally controlled. While these mobilizations typically are conceptualized as apolitical pranks (albeit sometimes on a large scale involving thousands of people), they have also been seen as a new form of sociability that can inspire new forms of political protest.[7]

Whether flash mobs are a political statement, a marketing tool, or the mass mobilization of fun, the phenomenon results from the ability of large numbers of individuals to connect with each other; they engage each other and share information in an online public forum. Social network sites provide a quick and easy way to access information that is of relevance to the user. Groups created on social network sites for collective action can be frivolous (a simultaneous pillow fight in twenty-five cities around the globe) or very serious, such as the group One Million Voices Against FARC (Revolutionary Armed Forces of Colombia — People's Army), which is dedicated to stopping the guerrilla group deemed responsible for holding 750 hostages in the jungle.[8] Facebook groups have even been used to put pressure on Facebook.com itself to pursue a particular policy direction. For example, the Greenpeace International page, which claims to have mobilized four hundred thousand members in six weeks, wants Facebook to reverse its February 2010 decision to build a data centre in Oregon that is powered by coal, which environmentalists say is the dirtiest form of energy. Or, witness the growth of the group "Petition: Facebook, respect my privacy!" that gathered a hundred thousand members in just over a week. When combined with "tweets" and cellphone text messages, these pages provide a powerful "word of mouth" venue where like-minded people can gather in cyberspace.[9]

The use of social networking sites to disseminate information and mobilize international support is particularly significant in countries that use oppression to stifle dissent. In Myanmar (Burma), government forces brutally suppressed the so-called Saffron Revolution in 2007; this protest included the participation of Buddhist monks wearing their traditional saffron robes. While the Burmese government was successful in blocking access to the Internet within the country, it was unable to prevent activists outside the country from using the Facebook page "Support the Monks' Protest in Burma" to mobilize the Global Action Day for Burma on 6 October 2007.[10] The event "went viral" (that is, news of it circulated at an explosive rate), ultimately involving demonstrations in almost one hundred cities located in thirty countries. The site itself features posts from supporters around the world, including links to newspaper articles in their home countries and videos smuggled out of Burma.

A similar tale unfolded in Iran's controversial presidential elections in June 2009. Some referred to this as the "Green Revolution" because of the opposition party's use of green as its official colour, but many dubbed it the "Twitter Revolution." Many Iranians disputed the legitimacy of this election, and attempts by the government of Iran to suppress dissent failed. This was largely due to the use of cellphones to send instant messages containing locations of protests and the use of social networking to post information, including videos taken from cellphones. A dramatic example of a cellphone video that galvanized support for the dissidents is one that shows a young woman dying after being shot in the heart. Neda Agha-Soltan had been caught in a traffic jam caused by a protest. At the time of her death, she was standing beside her music teacher on the side of the road watching events unfold.[11] Opposition forces claimed that a government Basij militia sniper killed Agha-Soltan. This gruesome video also went viral, quickly circulating on the Internet and appearing on news networks worldwide. In response to the proliferation of texts and images that discredited its regime, the Iranian government created a "cyber army" that went on the counterattack using the same tools as the dissidents. The cyber army sought to block opposition communications and to track down opposition members through their use of the web. In this particular conflict, control of the web was deemed critical by both sides.[12] The Iranian attempt to shut down social networking was emulated by Egypt in 2011 when it was dealing with its own internal strife.[13] Control of the web means control of information, once again highlighting the importance of information access to governance.

The power of social networking sites to engage citizens in the political process is becoming increasingly important in liberal democratic nations as well. President Barack Obama's 2008 campaign capitalized on the significant change in media consumption habits over the past decade, specifically the decline of TV and newspapers as a source of news for many Americans and the subsequent rise in importance of the Internet. His campaign made extensive use of social networking, including niche market pages targeting particular groups on Facebook, including women, gays, and students. Obama's emphasis on organizing from the grassroots upward proved to be a natural fit with new peer-to-peer technologies that emphasize decentralized engagement. According to the Pew Internet and American Life Project nearly one-fifth of Internet users in 2008 posted comments on a blog, social networking site, website, or other online forums. The study also discovered that two-thirds of Americans between the ages of eighteen and twenty-four with a social networking account participated in some form of online political activity.[14] Should these trends continue, one would expect that social networking will become critical in the dissemination of information and the engagement of citizens in the political process.

The preceding illustrates the tremendous effectiveness of online social networking for peer-to-peer communication and for allowing access to particular forms of information. In that sense, networking is an important new tool in the access-to-information toolkit. But social networking also poses huge challenges for the protection of personal information. Facebook has recently gained much bad press because of changes to the site that facilitate the tracking of user activities and the sharing of this information without express consent. While the site does have privacy controls, they are so complex that most users are easily thwarted from protecting their personal information, if they are even sophisticated enough in their understanding of the issues to be paying attention. Threats to privacy on Facebook were exposed as early as 2005; two students at MIT conducted a comprehensive study of the privacy implications of Facebook as a class project. At that time, Facebook was confined to post-secondary students. They astutely noted: "Privacy on Facebook is undermined by three principal factors: users disclose too much, Facebook does not take adequate steps to protect user privacy, and third parties are actively seeking out end-user information using Facebook."[15] These three issues are interconnected. While many users are very careful with respect to what they post, more still are not, forgetting that what they post is seen not just by the particular person to whom the post was directed, but also by everyone who is their Facebook friend. Moreover, if they have not set their privacy settings to limit who sees their accounts, their information could potentially be seen by anyone with an Internet connection.

Overexposure of personal information on Facebook takes many forms. Many users include their birthdate in their profile, as Facebook will then send a reminder to their friends to wish them a happy birthday. Yet a birthdate (including the year of birth) is a key piece of personal information that is very useful to identity thieves; if they can combine it with a name and a postal code, such thieves are able to compromise bank accounts and credit cards. Similarly, many users do not limit access to their Facebook photo albums. Posting photo albums is a very convenient way to share pictures with family and friends who may live anywhere in the world. The tag feature is a quick and easy way of alerting friends to photos that would be of interest to them. But most users are unaware that Facebook's default for photo albums is "global"; anyone with access to a particular picture has access to the entire album. Access typically comes when a friend tags a person in a photo; the tagged photo is posted on the wall of the person who is tagged. Anyone who has access to the tagged person's wall can simply click on the photo, and unless the privacy settings in the album have been changed from the global default, the other pictures in the album are also accessible. The ability of Facebook users to see information provided by their friends has become an invaluable way to connect, reconnect, and maintain and deepen relationships among people. But it also has the potential for exposing personal information to complete strangers and to others who might use it for nefarious purposes.

Sharing of information with strangers is not the only problem, however. A Facebook "friend" can refer to a whole range of relationships, including family members, friends in the traditional sense of the term, acquaintances, classmates, and colleagues. It can also refer to a person with whom a person shares a common interest — be it a hobby, a religious commitment, or a political belief. Profile pages can be useful for networking purposes, and events are easily organized through the creation of a page that can serve not only to provide information but also to issue invitations. Profile pages are also used by organizations for a multitude of purposes. A university program might post a page to market itself or encourage interaction among its students. A politician might maintain a page in order to get her message out to supporters. An environmental lobby group might use its page to alert members to upcoming events in their community. The possibilities are endless in terms of the types of profiles that can be created; information can be circulated easily and without cost beyond the small investment of time it takes to create the page. Given the many advantages with respect to information access, transparency, and fun, it is little wonder that the popularity of social networking tools has exploded.

But consider for a moment the the case where a college student drinks too much one night and the event is caught in a photo. The photo is posted to Facebook and tagged so that it shows up on the student's profile page for all to see. The student might think that there is no problem — she is a new user and thus has a small circle of Facebook friends, only six in fact. Those six friends happened to be with her in the bar, so her cyberfriends are already aware that she had too much to drink that night. But the person who posted the picture has a far larger circle of Facebook friends (say, over two hundred), which might include the student's employer, a professor, or her aunt. The photo appears in the poster's news feed, making it accessible to her two hundred friends. To make matters worse, if the poster has not taken any of the steps necessary to limit access to the photo album from that night, a far greater number might have access to the photo. If the photo poster has tagged the other five friends who appear in photos in the same album, these photos will appear in the news feeds of not only the five tagged friends but also in the news feeds of all of their Facebook friends. Assuming the five friends have two hundred friends each (with no common friends), the tagged photos will be featured in the news feeds of an additional thousand people. Any of these people can click on the photo to gain access to the entire album, enabling them to view the action in the bar that Friday night. If they wish, they can download interesting photos to their desktops and send them to their contacts as email attachments. Moreover, if any of the picture poster's friends post comments on the wall of the picture, their comments will appear on the news feeds of all of their friends. These friends will now have access to the photo album: if five of the poster's friends comment on the wall of the photo and each of them has two hundred friends, another one thousand people will have access to the photos. As is often the case with the "friends of friends scenario," if the poster's two hundred friends, or the tagged friends' one thousand friends, or the five commenters' one thousand friends happen to include a someone who is also a Facebook friend of the college student's mother (like the student's aunt), the student might find herself explaining to her parents why she was photographed half-naked crouched over a toilet bowl. What boggles the mind even more is the realization that these numbers are based on users having two hundred Facebook friends; many young adults have double or triple that number.

It is not only college students, however, who are sometimes guilty of such indiscreet behaviour. Often unwittingly, parents follow suit. For example, many Facebook profiles feature photos of a new baby or young child posted by a proud mother, who tags a friend who happens to appear in the photo. The picture is just one of many in an album of photos that the mother has posted to her Facebook account; it hasn't occurred to her to change the default privacy setting for photo albums. Many of the mother's friends have already viewed the photo album and have posted comments on the mini-walls under the pictures, identifying not only the baby but other children who appear in the family photos. In addition, some posts mention the city in which the family lives or, for instance, the name of the elementary school that the baby's older sister attends. The proud mother wants one of her friends to see the picture, and she happily tags the friend so that the picture will be posted to the friend's wall. But does she really want the friends of her friend looking at the picture? Does she really want people she has never met downloading the picture simply by dragging the picture onto their computer desktop? And what if the friend allows global access to his or her account, allowing anyone with a Facebook account to see the picture and indeed the entire album? One challenge with privacy protection is that often people do not even realize that their privacy has been compromised.

The irony of this scene is that it is played out daily by parents who dutifully warn their children not to talk to strangers while walking down the street, who keep the family computer in a central location in order to monitor its use, and who block their children's access to particular websites in order to keep them safe online. But many of these same parents think nothing of posting pictures of their children to an online environment, accompanied by revealing information that makes these children vulnerable to predators. More fundamentally, however, a picture of a child posted on a parent's Facebook page immediately robs that child of a degree of personal autonomy. That is, a very young child does not consent to having his picture posted online; this choice is not his to make. Once the picture is posted it becomes the property of Facebook; even if the parent deletes the picture, the album, or even the entire account, Facebook retains the rights to that photo. As such, the child will never regain control of his image and must live with the lifetime consequences of his parents giving away his information when he was a minor. Those who have access to the photo can easily download it. As the default for photo albums is "everyone," many parents are in fact sharing this photo with anyone who has an Internet connection; it can be used for whatever purpose the downloader decides is appropriate. Obviously if the downloaders happen to be pedophiles, their definition of what is "appropriate" may not align with the person whose image they now have in their possession.

Online communities constitute another form of engagement: they provide social and political outlets that were not possible before the invention of the Internet. They also allow for new forms of political and social engagement that are not subject to control by gatekeepers who exercise power in a vertical, top-down fashion. The interests of the user determine who users interact with. But the very power of peer-to-peer relationships should give pause to those engaged in them, as sometimes this engagement comes at great expense to personal privacy. This is not to say that an individual should avoid participating in social networking activities, only that the individual should consciously choose what personal information to reveal to the world. Though individuals might not realize it, through the release of this information the individual is creating a digital identity that once formed can be difficult to change.

DIGITAL IDENTITIES, THE COMMODIFICATION OF PERSONALITY, AND THE BACKLASH

Social networking involves the creation of an online identity that is accessible to a variety of people for a variety of purposes. Users create online identities for the purposes of meeting others with similar interests, for dating or companionship, for sexual encounters, or for professional promotion. The types of information posted on these sites will vary according to the purpose of the poster and will be used according to the needs of those who access it: the wealth of information on these sites is an extremely valuable commodity for companies to use for marketing purposes, for law enforcement agencies, and for others. Few people who post information on these sites read the "terms and agreement" section of the sign-up page, nor do they read the site's privacy policy. Thus they remain ignorant of how social networking sites use their data. In addition, they may not have put much thought into which users should have access to their digital identity and what the negative aspects are of losing control of this identity.

Studies indicate that men and women use social networking sites differently. Women typically use social networks to share personal information, discuss day-to-day activities, and to deepen relationships, while men use them to promote themselves and to share ideas for the purpose of self-advancement. Women are more likely to feel vulnerable to stalkers and abusive ex-partners, and, predictably, studies indicate that women are more concerned than men about how personal information might be used in ways that compromise their safety. In other words, they are generally more risk-averse.[16] Facebook's recent trouble with its privacy policy has led to the assertion that "Facebook Is a Feminist Issue." As one writer pointed out on the *Geek Feminism Blog*, unless you run your own server, using social media requires you to store personal information on someone else's server.[17] The owner of that server determines how your information will be used. By extension, the owner of that server also has control over that part of your digital identity that is stored on the server. As mentioned previously, anything posted on Facebook becomes the property of Facebook, whether or not the user deletes it from her account. Thus the issue of control of a person's digital identity is not one that is limited to the "now" but extends indefinitely into the future.

New Facebook procedures and changes to its privacy policy have provoked a huge backlash among users. Initially, the site allowed access to a user's information only to members of groups specified by the user. Over the years, however, Facebook has incrementally chipped away at privacy. Defaults that were initially set as "friends only" were changed to "everyone," the option to keep certain information private was taken away, and user-controlled privacy settings became increasingly complex and difficult to use. Whenever privacy changes provoked user anger, Facebook acknowledged the dissatisfaction by restoring privacy, but never quite to the same level as it had been previously. This reflects a growing trend toward the commodification of identity for profit. Personal information is a valuable resource that, when sold to advertisers, can generate unimaginable profit for those who control the information. As one technology blogger lamented:

> What we are seeing now is a result of the commodification of personality which, in late capitalism, creates value for corporates. We are all unpaid labourers in the social media industry, whose lives are fodder for the accumulation of capital. Facebook profits from our sociality.[18]

What this blogger does not mention is that the social network's unpaid labourers give up their information willingly, even enthusiastically. With almost half a billion users in 2010 providing a virtually limitless source of information, it is worth contemplating that when Facebook CEO Mark Zuckerberg was asked in 2003 why fellow Harvard students would willingly send him four thousand emails, pictures, address, and Social Security numbers, he allegedly responded in an instant message session: "I don't know why. They 'trust me.' Dumb f**cks." [19] Facebook does not deny the authenticity of this widely reported exchange, which was reputedly leaked by a Silicon Valley insider. Zuckerberg has been heavily criticized for his cavalier attitude. If Zuckerberg did in fact say this, it would seem that Facebook's CEO is a typical digital native — one who, now in a professional position, may wish he had exercised more discretion when using instant messaging technologies at the age of nineteen.

The commodification of information is particularly noticeable with Facebook applications that allow third party access to the personal information of the user. Applications, or "apps," are installed by the user and take the form of quizzes, games, polls, booklists, friend and car pool organizers — the list is endless. Games such as Zynga's "Farmville" and "Mafia Wars" are big business: the company boasts 235 million monthly active gamers and 65 million daily gamers. [20] Facebook provides the platform to play the Zynga game. In May 2010, Zynga and Facebook announced a five-year "strategic partnership" that would see gamers able to use Facebook credits in Zynga games. While games can be played for free, progress in the game depends on virtual money that is either earned through the user's activity in the game or purchased with a credit card. Acquiring virtual money is where gamers expose themselves to risk — they may find that the survey they took to win currency subscribes them (for a monthly fee) to a horoscope service, or they may find that accepting a gift or responding to a request exposes them to hackers or viruses. [21] But most unsettling for those who wish to maintain control over their personal privacy is that when a user installs applications, Facebook allows the same access rights that the user set for other users accessing his account. If these access rights were left at the "everyone" default, the user gives the applications access to all of his personal information. As of spring 2010, Facebook's privacy policy was almost 6,000 words long and users needed to look at 50 different settings and chose among 170 options to change Facebook's latest default settings. Users can control what data an application can access, but it is a complicated task and for the vast majority of users is not easily accomplished. Moreover, many users do not realize that Facebook has changed its privacy settings, or if they do, they may not fully grasp the implications of the change.

What is particularly troubling, however, is that Facebook gives applications access to the gamer's friends' information as well. So, while a particular user might not expose his information by using Facebook applications, he must also set his privacy settings to prohibit the sharing of his information with applications. If he does not do this, his friends who take quizzes, sign up for polls, and play online games put his information at risk. Many Facebook users complained when the news feed was introduced because it broadcast their network activities to all of their friends; some did not wish to have their activities tracked and publicized. Later, users began to object to the large volume of information they were receiving in their news feeds from their friends who are heavy users of applications. Users' broadcasted activities include things such as progress on various games or the results of the quiz they just took. The constant updates are not only a source of irritation, they also leave the friend of the heavy user wondering if the gamer/quiz taker has larger problems that are morphing into social networking addiction issues. One advantage of the news feed, however, is that it provides information as to which of a user's friends most frequently engages in activities that could compromise a user's online privacy.

In April 2010, Facebook created Community Pages, which are devoted to a particular activity as opposed to being connected to a particular organization. Users can create their own community pages; however, Facebook created the vast majority of these pages using Wikipedia entries as placeholders. Fields in user profiles are automatically linked to these community pages. So, for example, many users include in their profiles their hometowns, current city, schools attended, employers, and interests. These are automatically linked to the associated community page and the user will be listed on this page as liking the organization, activity, or place. Facebook states that the goal of the community pages "is to make them the best collection of shared knowledge on a topic."[22] But what this means for many users is that, unbeknownst to them, they may be listed as "liking" a community page that they did not know existed because they listed an interest on their profiles. One telling example of this is the honour roll high school student whose parents are worried about the amount of time he spends playing video games. Poking fun at his parents' concern, the student lists "And Play Video Games, I'm a Terrible Person" under "interests" on Facebook. The student is listed as liking the community page "And Play Video Games." The student might not object to this, as he does indeed enjoy playing video games. But he probably would not like the fact that he is also listed (along with his profile photo) as liking the community group "I'm a Terrible Person," which features a news feed of status updates from a variety of people who appear to have problems with depression. Here again, the changes that Facebook made to its layout and to its privacy policy are not well understood, despite the vociferous backlash that erupted prompting well-known technology luminaries to delete their accounts.

The development and linking of community pages to user profiles reflects a trend toward privacy erosion that has been consistent since Facebook's inception. In 2005, Facebook assured users that their personal information would be available only to those users belonging to specified groups. The following year, the default of "specified groups" changed to users' schools, local area, and other "reasonable" communities. The next year, a specified group was expanded to a network that included "friends of friends." By 2009, the default had shifted from privacy to access. In the words of Facebook, the "everyone" default was designed

> to make it easy for you to share your information with anyone you want. Information set to "everyone" is publicly available information, may be accessed by everyone on the Internet (including people not logged into Facebook), is subject to indexing by third party search engines, may be associated with you outside of Facebook (such as when you visit other sites on the internet), and may be imported and exported by us and others without privacy limitations.[23]

The following month, Facebook announced that certain categories of information (such as name, gender, geographic location, and fan pages) would be made publicly available and as such would not be subject to privacy settings. Additionally, it announced that user information would be shared with selected third parties. This culminated in the 2010 announcement that various bits of information contained on a user's profile would be transformed into "connections" to community pages, as would clicking the "like" button on a webpage, thus causing it to appear on the news feeds of the user's friends.[24]

The uproar over Facebook's privacy policy prompted US senators to petition the Federal Trade Commission to provide guidelines for social networking sites. According to a press release from the office of Senator Charles E. Schumer, the appeal to the FTC followed reports that

> Facebook has decided to provide user data to select third party websites and has begun sharing personal profile information that users previously had the ability to restrict access to. These recent changes by Facebook fundamentally change the relationship between the user and the social networking site....And there is little guidance on what social networking sites can and cannot do and what disclosures are necessary to consumers.[25]

The senators' intervention followed a complaint about Facebook's privacy policy to the Federal Trade Commission by ten organizations concerned about online privacy, including the Electronic Privacy Information Center, the Electronic Frontier Foundation, and the American Civil Liberties Union.

The senators were not the first to complain about Facebook's privacy policies; in fact, the United States is a latecomer to the party. In August 2009, the Canadian Internet Policy and Public Interest Clinic made a detailed complaint to Canada's privacy commissioner concerning Facebook's complex and convoluted privacy policies that spoke to issues of data retention, security safeguards, and whether users were provided with sufficient information to give informed consent. After conducting an investigation, the commissioner dismissed some parts of the complaint, but did find Facebook to be in contravention of Canadian privacy law:

> Facebook did not have adequate safeguards in place to prevent unauthorized access by application developers to users' personal information, and furthermore was not doing enough to ensure that meaningful consent was obtained from individuals for the disclosure of their personal information to application developers.[26]

The commissioner proposed corrective measures, and in August 2009 the investigating officer for the case reported:

> Facebook is promising to make significant technological changes to address the issue we felt was the biggest risk for users — the relatively free flow of personal information to more than one million application developers around the world. . . . Application developers have had virtually unrestricted access to Facebook users' personal information. The changes Facebook plans to introduce will allow users to control the types of personal information that applications can access.[27]

Six months later, the privacy commissioner was investigating the privacy implications of Facebook's introduction of Community Pages because of another complaint.

On 21 April 2009, Mark Zuckerberg once again raised eyebrows when he stated at the F8 Developer Conference that Facebook is "building a Web where the default is social." As one technology commentator observed: "To our ears, that sounds like 'a Web where exposure is the norm.'" [28] The following month, the Article 29 Data Protection Working Group (comprised of the European Union's data protection agencies) sent a letter to Facebook that said: "It is unacceptable that the company fundamentally changed the default settings on its social-networking platform to the detriment of a user." The group sent similar letters to twenty other social networking sites that are signatories to the "Safer Networking Principles for the EU." In its letters, the group emphasized the importance of gaining the explicit consent of social networking users before sharing their information with search engines or with third-party application developers. The Canadian privacy commissioner also waded into the fray, openly musing about a fresh Facebook investigation. A spokesperson for her office complained, "Although they've done some things right, in a few areas, they seem to have gone in the opposite direction and that's been disappointing." These events led a Canadian research chair in Internet and e-commerce law to observe in 2010: "This is getting ugly. Facebook badly overreached last December and they have been very slow to respond to the mounting criticism. I think we will see regulatory and court actions in multiple jurisdictions by the end of the year." [29]

At the outset of this discussion, it was observed that few social network users understand the implications of a poorly managed digital identity. This is understandable given the complexity of the privacy policies of social networking sites like Facebook. It is even more understandable given that a Facebook account is only one component of a person's digital identity. This identity is comprised of a multitude of other components that are created every time a consumer buys something online, blogs, tweets, or posts a comment on a discussion board. These data can be matched with other data, creating a composite picture of a person. The question for privacy advocates is: How and by whom should this identity be controlled?

THE FUTURE OF FACEBOOK

The jury is still out with respect to how Facebook will respond to its critics. It is also anyone's guess as to whether or not Facebook users will "vote with their feet" by quitting the site altogether. To this end, two Canadians started a website "quitfacebook.com" wherein users commit to deleting their accounts on 31 May 2010. In less than a month, the group reported over twenty thousand members. This number is a fraction of the almost half a billion Facebook users, but the speed with which the twenty thousand users were mobilized once again demonstrates the ability of the Internet to connect people with issues. In its May 2010 survey of visitors to its site, the UK-based security firm Sophos reported that 60 percent claimed that they were considering quitting Facebook because of privacy concerns. By its own admission, the Sophos poll is biased toward those who already are sensitized to privacy and security issues by virtue of the fact that they were visiting the Sophos website. Nonetheless, even those who work at Sophos seemed surprised by the results. One of its senior technology consultants opined:

> I think for people who work in the IT security field, it's becoming harder and harder to justify being on Facebook. . . . The number of privacy problems are making more people realize that it may not be where they want to be. Of course, some people may simply reduce the amount of data that they publish on the site rather than quit. The average guy on the street, meanwhile, will probably need a bigger push to quit the site.[30]

While it is impossible to know how many people will eventually quit the social networking site, in May 2010 Google Canada reported that the most widely used search term in relation to Facebook was "delete account." Statistics from Google also showed that, internationally, the number of users looking for information regarding deleting their accounts had jumped by 3.6 million in the space of only three days.[31] Given that Facebook and Google are in a pitched battle for dominance of the web (with hits to Facebook surpassing those to Google for the first time in March 2010), one might question the accuracy of these numbers, given that Google produces them. As was noted in the previous chapter, Google is also in the spotlight with its own privacy scandal after it was discovered that the cameras collecting pictures for Google Street View were accidently collecting personal data from unsecured home WiFi networks as well. Presumably, then, any opportunity for Google to divert attention to the privacy woes of another major online service provider would be welcome. That said, there is no doubt that in the spring of 2010 the web was abuzz with chatter about alternatives to Facebook such as Diaspora, an open-source personal web server.

What one is left to conclude from this brief overview of Facebook is that online communications are profoundly changing not only the way in which we communicate but also the value of personal identity. Peer-to-peer communication places a premium on personal autonomy — it allows users to communicate independently and to form and re-form messages according to users' perceptions and values. This breaks down hierarchy by allowing a bottom-up construction of social and political reality, as opposed to relying on traditional sources of news where power is concentrated at the top and communication is disseminated downward. As Manuel Castells notes: "The wide availability of individually controlled wireless communication effectively bypasses the mass-media system as a source of information, and creates a new form of public space." [32] These observations are equally applicable to social networking.

New public spaces are increasingly virtual; they are places where like-minded individuals from all over the globe can meet, communicate, and strategize. As such, social networking provides an important tool for accessing the information that is so critically important to democratization efforts. The ability to mobilize large numbers of people quickly has been demonstrated in a variety of jurisdictions; these mobilizations have even been successful in countries where repressive regimes have gone to great lengths to block communication through social networking. One only needs to look at Burma, Iran, and Egypt for evidence of the difficulties encountered by centralized authorities in trying to stifle the dissemination of information by individuals to a global audience using peer-to-peer technologies. The election of President Obama also illustrates the utility of using peer-to-peer technologies for grassroots mobilization in support of a politician.

Like the medical information and surveillance technologies that were discussed in previous chapters, social networking presents serious challenges for the protection of information privacy. In the case of social networking, the problem is compounded by the fact that the organizations gathering the information are in the private sector, and as such, this information (and indeed, personal identity) is an important commodity that is worth a substantial sum of money. Moreover, social networking is such a new phenomenon that the average person really does not understand the implications of its use for personal autonomy. Nor do most individuals understand how their information can be used for profit or for fraudulent purposes. Even individuals who understand the complex issues around privacy are hard pressed to exercise their freedom to quit using social networking tools. As James Grimmelmann notes:

> Facebook provides users with a forum in which they can craft social identities, forge reciprocal relationships, and accumulate social capital. These are important, even primal, human desires, whose immediacy can trigger systematic biases in the mechanisms that people use to evaluate privacy risks.[33]

Moreover, more and more individuals and organizations are using tools like Facebook as the communicative vehicle of choice. In the very near future, deleting a Facebook account may become akin to committing social and professional suicide — with consequences similar to those for the North American family that chooses to possess neither land lines nor cellphones. A generous view of this family would categorize the parents as anti-social; a less generous view would claim that the parents are behaving irresponsibly in voluntarily cutting themselves and their children off from the rest of the world.

If it is indeed true that social networks represent "public space" then very careful consideration needs to be given to who controls that public space and how the power within that space is exercised. Returning to the central theme of this book, the essential questions become: What should the balance be between the right to privacy versus the right to access personal information? Is social networking sufficiently important to both personal autonomy and to larger society that it should not be left entirely up to either market forces or individual choice? Is there a place for government intervention or even control of social networking sites? If this is the case, what limits should be put on public intervention?

CH_7
*Balancing Freedom of Information
and the Protection of Privacy*

Information and communication technologies (ICTs) have revolutionized the way in which we communicate. The ubiquitous use of email, cellphones, digital cameras, instant messaging, and social networking allows people to share information instantly and to connect, reconnect, and stay connected with people all over the globe in ways that were inconceivable a mere decade ago. At the same time, the ever-increasing ability of computer technology to collect, store, retrieve, and transmit information is dramatically changing how commerce and governance is conducted. Organizations collect massive amounts of data (in word and pictorial form) concerning our activities as both citizens and consumers. This gives rise to privacy concerns; in particular, how can individuals control what is known about themselves? But ICTs also provide opportunity for fostering social and political engagement, enhancing service, facilitating trade, and increasing security. While it is reasonable to worry about the possibility of "Big Brother" knowing everything about you, the "knowing" can work in both directions: ICTs also allow the individual citizen-consumer to scrutinize government and other large organizations in ways that were not possible a few years ago. There might be good reasons for an organization to seek to suppress information, but as this becomes more difficult, government, corporate, and nonprofit accountability will undoubtedly increase.

Social scientists in the coming decades will be confronted with two vexing questions. How will ICTs change the nature of the relationship between citizens and government? How will ICTs change the relationship between the citizen-consumer and others in society with either complementary or competing interests? The analysis of competing interests is central to the discipline of political science, which concerns itself with the distribution of power. But these issues will touch the lives of many professionals from a wide range of disciplines. Sociologists, legal scholars, and philosophers have waded into the murky waters of the privacy debate to assess the challenges new technologies pose for the ability of citizen-consumers to control their personal information. Scholars with an interest in human rights and public administration have looked at the relationship between transparency and democratic governance. They have considered how dissidents use new devices for surveillance and communication to counter hegemonic thought or to promote larger organizational accountability. Still others have examined the legislative framework that underpins privacy and transparency. The difficulty is that the technologies and the issues are changing so quickly that studies become dated shortly after they are completed.

The intersection of freedom of information (FOI) and the protection of privacy should be of great interest beyond the scholarly community as well; these issues impact everyone. The issues, however, are so complex and the technology for digitizing government, commerce, and communications is changing at such a rapid pace that it is virtually impossible for social science analysis to keep up. For the average person, the task of understanding the issues is verging on impossible. But unless we are content to be swept along by the forces of change, accepting whatever is given to us by those who have a particular interest (usually commercial) in the new technologies, we must at least attempt to keep our heads above water. We might even decide to swim across the current and head for shore.

Governments collect massive amounts of data concerning their citizens. As taxpayers who pay for the collection of this information, and indeed for the operations of government generally, citizens are entitled to know what their governments are doing and what information they hold. Consumers want to know the same things. Though they might not have the same rights to access information regarding the internal workings of a company as citizens with respect to governments, they certainly should have the ability to determine whether or not the company is operating within the regulatory framework that is set out in legislation. The ability to access information ensures accountability, which hinges on two old chestnuts of public administration: fixed rules and due process. Put more plainly, both consumers and citizens should be able to track the activities of large organizations in order to eradicate, or at least inhibit, corruption by ensuring that those organizations are operating within the law.

Unfortunately for the citizen-consumer, there can be great administrative resistance to any attempt to create a regime of free-flowing information. This is not always a result of corruption or other wrongdoing. It can be the result of a lack of resources provided to those in charge of managing information, making it very difficult for them to effectively perform their mandated role. It also can be the result of ignorance of the actual purpose of freedom of information laws. Clearly, those whose roles include responsibility for responding to access requests would benefit from training and sufficient resources to fulfill their obligations.

What is troublesome for critics of a vision of the world where information flows freely is their suspicion that the riches will not be distributed evenly and that existing inequities will be reinforced. Those who are in the position to collect and manipulate information will benefit from the flow far more than others with limited or no access. Thus, existing inequities could be exacerbated between countries in the northern and southern hemispheres, corporations and consumers, socio-economic classes, anglophones and speakers of other languages, and the mainstream and the marginalized. These concerns ultimately relate to larger issues of control of the Internet and of intellectual property. Who controls information and knowledge?

Of equal importance to the creation of a FOI regime is the protection of privacy. Privacy in many respects is an even more complex concept than transparency and as such is difficult to define. At its most basic, however, it speaks to the autonomy of the individual, specifically the right to be left alone to pursue one's self-interest without interference. It includes the need for confidentiality; without this, professionals in the legal and health fields could not develop the relationship of trust with their clients that they need if they are to provide effective service. Similarly, there is a place for secrecy in some organizational activities: a measure of secrecy can be necessary for commercial success and for security. Though it is tempting to juxtapose simplistically the right of an individual for privacy with the right of the group to advance the interest of the majority of people within a society, ultimately a measure of privacy for the individual is in the best interest of the group. Total transparency is "too much of a good thing," and so is total privacy.

Efforts to balance privacy and transparency can be seen in the proliferation of both FOI and privacy regimes around the world. Legislative initiatives are a result of new technologies for collecting, storing, and disseminating information, of the rise of e-commerce activities that use electronic information, of the ability to create comprehensive information profiles by matching data, and of the sheer amount of information that is being collected. But the biggest challenge to privacy ultimately comes from the private sector; there is a great deal of money to be made from access to our personal information. While the differences among legislative regimes reflect both the time and place in which they were developed, generally speaking, regimes are converging as nations attempt to align their practices to facilitate trade.

Data management, of course, is not just restricted to written records: there are many types of data derived from other sources. This book has considered not only the printed word but also the sharing of medical images such as X-rays, photographic images produced from cellphones, cameras, and video cameras, and locational information obtained from GPS devices. The issues around the collection, retention, and use of information are complex and as varied as the technologies that allow their collection. As such, issues cannot be neatly divided into two silos of competing interests corresponding to access and privacy.

Thus far this book might seem to suggest that it is the ICTs themselves that are the single largest threat to privacy. An important factor in decreasing privacy is our willingness to give up our privacy in exchange for something else. Using Facebook to socialize, using loyalty cards to earn free products, and posting pictures or videos for the attention they draw are all examples of decisions that individuals make that compromise their privacy. Assuming that they have a basic understanding of the implications of their decisions, those making them have decided that the personal gain that they accrue from these activities is worth the privacy they lose.

But does this mean that the abdication of privacy necessarily guarantees an expectation of transparency or some other societal benefit? Clearly not, but of equal concern is the tendency of some to become "privacy pit bulls" who intuitively recognize the problems for individual autonomy associated with new ICT technologies but do not pay much attention to the use of data for the promotion of the public good. In this instance, the "public good" is most easily understood from a public administration perspective, where "transparency" implies access to information. Transparency can result in improved service delivery, increased security, and increased accountability. As is demonstrated in the discussion of health information, access to information can make very tangible improvements to patient treatment both in terms of service delivery and knowledge gained through medical research. Better methods for the detection and treatment of illness will save money because of shortened hospital stays, fewer days missed from work, and less unpaid familial outpatient care. All of these benefits, however, come at the expense of sharing what many consider their most private information.

Similarly, the chapters on surveillance and social networking argue that transparency and access to information are critical for ensuring democratic accountability, and in particular due process and participation. Transparency ensures the rule of law — that the rules of the game are clearly understood and followed. While the rules could arguably favour a particular group, at the very least the rules are visible, and as such, they can be debated. The chapter on social networking demonstrates how access to information can facilitate new forms of relationships, either peer-to-peer social networking or networking for the purpose of affecting political change. This new communication is fundamentally different from previous top-down forms of hierarchical communication and facilitates the engagement that is critical to both social cohesion and political participation. The accountability that transparency seeks to produce is seen as defining the public benefit of surveillance. Surveillance is used to increase public safety and to monitor the activities of individuals in the workplace (particularly with respect to police and military personnel). Surveillance is also used to increase efficiency and convenience in a variety of activities. As before, a critical question when examining these "public goods" is: What level of societal benefit must be evident to justify the infringement on privacy? Privacy, as its advocates are quick to point out, is central to a person's sense of personal space and security. It allows us a measure of control over what people know about us. In the end, the political community must determine the balance between privacy and transparency. Ultimately what is being asked is: What is the proper balance between the rights of individuals and those of the larger community that they live within?

This book argues that in the new millennium the dual areas of freedom of information and protection of privacy are of critical importance to the nature of the relationships between the citizen-consumer and large organizations (including but not limited to the state). The adage "knowledge is power" is particularly applicable in the information age: having (or not having) access to information and the knowledge associated with it will alter relationships of power. So too will the ability to keep information confidential, be it personal or organizational. ICTs are providing new opportunities for the undermining of autonomy through various forms of surveillance. At the same time, they offer a measure of personal empowerment, making it possible, for example, for an individual to connect easily with like-minded people for the purpose of keeping large organizations accountable. When using ICTs, though, most individuals focus on the benefits of "connection" without thinking about what is lost with respect to their individual autonomy. This point is of particular significance to so-called digital natives, who may find that the digital record of their youthful exuberance (or imprudence) can harm their employment or relationship prospects in the future.

One of the primary goals of this book has therefore been to underscore the importance of freedom of information and protection of privacy to social relationships. In doing so, it seeks to stimulate a thoughtful and self-reflective analysis of how the management of new technologies will define the roles and personal spaces of new graduates who are poised to take their places as citizen-consumers contributing both to the democratic process and to the market economy. In particular, this reflection will encourage all of us to analyze issues that have been debated for centuries: What does the ideal political community look like, and what implications does this ideal have for individual autonomy?

QUESTIONS FOR DISCUSSION

CH_1

1. What factors explain the growing importance of access to information and protection of privacy concerns?

2. What is the relationship between FOI and democracy?

3. What is the relationship between privacy and personal autonomy?

4. How do FOI and privacy conflict? Which is most important?

5. Outline the four types of transparency and explain how they can promote and detract from building a good and just society.

6. Outline the four components of privacy and explain how they relate to personal autonomy.

7. How can the diffusion of information privilege particular groups?

8. How does the relationship between access and privacy reflect the values of a given community?

CH_2

1. Explain the differences between privacy, confidentiality, and secrecy.

2. How does information privacy differ from other forms of privacy?

3. What factors are leading to heightened concern over privacy?

4. How are attitudes toward privacy shaped by culture, ideology, and epoch?

5. Explain how various groups in society are differentially affected by threats to privacy.

6. What are the problems surrounding "free choice" and "consent" with respect to privacy protection?

CH_3

1. What are the two components that underpin the right to freedom of information? Explain why citizens have this right.

2. How is FOI related to the concept of legitimacy in both the public and private sectors?

3. Why are FOI regimes particularly important to newly emerging democracies and what are some of the challenges associated with their implementation?

4. What are some of the challenges associated with implementing FOI regimes in established democracies?

5. How can these challenges be addressed?

6. Explain the instances where transparency can justifiably be trumped by privacy.

CH_ 4

1. Why is health information considered to be particularly sensitive?

2. What is an electronic health record? What are the benefits and problems associated with its use?

3. How do attitudes toward particular medical issues vary by society and over time? How do these attitudes affect the sharing of medical data?

4. Explain what is meant by the secondary use of information.

5. In what circumstances should the public benefit of sharing medical information override the privacy interest of the individual?

6. Are there instances when genetic profiling is justified?

CH_5

1. Explain the difference between panopticon and syn-opticon. Which will prevail as the dominant form of surveillance in years to come?

2. What are the benefits and costs of the mass diffusion of video technologies with respect to surveillance? Are the costs worth the benefits?

3. Explain why the lines are blurring between surveil-lance for private and public benefit. Which will prevail as the dominant form of surveillance in years to come?

4. In what circumstances should the public benefit of surveillance override the privacy interests of the individual?

5. How have new surveillance technologies changed the nature of transparency and accountability in the public and private sectors?

6. How and why is surveillance experienced differently by different groups of people?

CH_6

1. How have peer-to-peer communications changed both the way we communicate and how we relate to one another and to institutions?

2. How does this form of communication both enhance and diminish personal autonomy?

3. Do the benefits of peer-to-peer communication outweigh the disadvantages?

4. The "commodification" of personality refers to the collection of personal information to build a digital profile that can be bought or sold. Explain the various ways this commodity can be used to the advantage of the individual from whom the information derives, those who have access to that information, and those who control it.

5. To what extent should governments regulate the collection, storage, retention, and posting of information collected from social networking sites? In other words, should people in a virtual public space be protected from their own ignorance and/or imprudence?

6. Should governments have the ability to limit the actions of social networking sites that the state determines are harmful to society? Put another way, in what circumstances should the public benefit of regulating social media override the private interest of a deregulated environment?

CH_7

1. Explain how ICTs have influenced communication, service provision, trade, and security.

2. How can the management of ICTs change the nature of the relationship between citizens and government?

3. How can the management of ICTs change the relationship between the citizen-consumer and others in society with either complementary or competing interests?

4. Does the loss of privacy ensure transparency and vice versa? Explain why this is or is not the case.

5. How does the management of ICTs define societal relationships, and in particular, define the role of the individual(s) within a community?

NOTES

CH_1
An Introduction to Freedom of Information and the Protection of Privacy

1 Helen Margetts, "Transparency and Digital Government," in *Transparency: The Key to Better Governance?* ed. Christopher Hood and David Heald, 198.

2 For the most part, I will use the terms *freedom of information* and *access to information* interchangeably. That said, while *freedom of information* is a general term, applicable in a broad array of contexts, *access to information* tends to be used with reference to personal information, typically in electronic format, that is held by an organization.

3 Amitai Etzioni, *The Limits of Privacy*, 184.

4 See David Heald, "Varieties of Transparency," in *Transparency*, ed. Hood and Heald, 25–43. Note that, in relation to upwards and downwards transparency, Heald's typology can seem somewhat counter-intuitive in that it refers to the direction in which information flows rather than to the direction of sight, from watcher to watched. Thus, in upwards transparency, in which information flows from subordinates to superiors, the watcher is looking downwards. Similarly, in downwards transparency, those watching look upwards at those invested with authority.

5 David Heald, "Transparency as an Instrumental Value," in *Transparency*, ed. Hood and Heald, 71.

6 Privacy International, *Privacy and Human Rights 2000: Overview*, www.privacyinternational.org/survey/phr2000/overview.html (accessed 6 December 2010).

7 For a succinct review of some pre-twentieth-century ideas that link transparency to the rule of law and to morality, see Christopher Hood, "Transparency in Historical Perspective," in *Transparency*, ed. Hood and Heald, 5–10.

8 Catharine MacKinnon, *Toward a Feminist Theory of the State*, 194.

9 Ann Florini, "The End of Secrecy," in *Power and Conflict in the Age of Transparency*, ed. Bernard I. Finel and Kristin M. Lord, 52.

10 Universities are one example of public institutions that are struggling with this issue. Some students use networking sites such as juicycampus.com to slander professors, to cheat, and to spread rumours, sometimes quite vicious ones. There was a particularly ugly incident at one Canadian university, in which a student assumed the identity of a professor, posted a degrading, racist YouTube video, and then emailed it to other students. Incidents like this have led to calls for universities to impose sanctions on students who are behaving inappropriately — but this leads directly into the debate over where the boundary lies between a student's personal space and the institutional space of the university. See Tim Johnson, "The Wild Web," *University Affairs*, 6 October 2008, http://www.universityaffairs.ca/the-wild-web.aspx (accessed 18 March 2010).

11 Kristin M. Lord, *The Perils and Promise of Global Transparency: Why the Information Revolution May Not Lead to Security, Democracy, or Peace*, 4.

12 For these and other revealing statistics, see Internet World Stats: Usage and Population Statistics, http://www.internetworldstats.com/stats4.htm (for Europe) and http://www.internetworldstats.com/stats1.htm (for Africa) (accessed 4 June 2011).

13 Similar debates over who should control information and knowledge production have arisen in the area of copyright law, as
well as in connection with the open access movement, which
seeks to make information freely available (thereby undercut-
ting traditional business models), and the open source initiative,
which allows users to adapt software code to suit their own
purposes. The crux of the debate has to do with the desire to
de-commodify information, which opponents of freely circulating information regard as a financial threat.

CH_2
Privacy Protection

1 See "Blatter's Remarks About Women's Soccer Uniforms Draw
Reax," *SportsBusinessDaily*, 19 January 2004, http://www.sports
businessdaily.com/article/82103 (accessed 8 January 2011).

2 Anita L. Allen, *Uneasy Access: Privacy for Women in a Free Society*, 3.

3 Samuel Warren and Louis D. Brandeis, "The Right to Privacy,"
Harvard Law Review 4 (1890): 193.

4 Zelman Cowen, *The Private Man: The Boyer Lectures, 1969*, 9–10.

5 Australian Law Reform Commission, *For Your Information: Australian Privacy Law and Practice*, vol. 1, sec. 15.109, p. 561 (also at
sec. 13.34, p. 492), http://www.austlii.edu.au/au/other/alrc/
publications/reports/108/ (accessed 10 April 2010).

6 Ibid. sec. 15.110, p. 561.

7 See United Nations, "The Universal Declaration of Human
Rights," G.A. res. 217A (III), U.N. Doc. A/810 (1948), Article 12;
United Nations, "International Covenant on Civil and Political
Rights," G.A. res. 2200A (XXI), U.N. Doc. A/6316 (1966), 999 U.N.T.S.
171, Article 17; and United Nations, "Convention on the Rights
of the Child," G.A. res. 44/25 (1989), Article 16; see also Council

of Europe, "European Convention on Human Rights" (1955), 312 U.N.T.S. 221, Article 8.

8 Electronic Privacy Information Centre and Privacy International, *Privacy and Human Rights 2002: An International Survey of Privacy Laws and Developments*, www.privacyinternational.org/survey/ phr2002/phr2002-part1.pdf (accessed 12 April 2010).

9 *R. v. Dyment*, [1988] 2 S.C.R. 417, at 427–28.

10 Canada, Department of Communications and Department of Justice, Task Force on Privacy and Computers, *Privacy and Computers: A Report of a Task Force Established Jointly by Dept. of Communications/Dept. of Justice*, 13.

11 Alan F. Westin, *Privacy and Freedom*, 7.

12 Michael Kirby, "Privacy Protection, a New Beginning: OECD Principles Twenty Years On," *Privacy Law and Policy Reporter* 6, no. 3 (1999): 25.

13 "OECD Council Recommendation," in Organisation for Economic Co-operation and Development, *Guidelines on the Protection of Privacy* (1980), http://www.oecd.org/document/18/0,3746,en_2649 _34255_1815186_1_1_1_1,00.html (accessed 12 February 2011).

14 General Provisions, Article 1, "Object of the Directive," in European Union, *Directive 95/46/EC of the European Parliament and of the Council of 24 October 1995 on the Protection of Individuals with Regard to the Processing of Personal Data and on the Free Movement of Such Data* (1995), O.J.L. 281/31, http://eur-lex.europa.eu/LexUriServ/ LexUriServ.do?uri=CELEX:31995L0046:en:html (accessed 18 March 2010).

15 Asia-Pacific Economic Cooperation, *APEC Privacy Framework* (2005), "Preamble," http://www.apec.org/Press/News-Releases /2005/~/media/Files/Press/NewsRelease/2005/04_amm_014rev1. ashx (accessed 3 June 2011).

16 Johanna G. Tan, "A Comparative Study of the APEC Privacy Framework — a New Voice in the Data Protection Dialogue?" *Asian Journal of Comparative Law* 3, no. 1, article 7 (2008) (accessed 12 February 2011). See also Graham Greenleaf, "Australia's APEC Privacy Initiative: The Pros and Cons of 'OECD Lite,'" *Privacy Law and Policy Reporter* 10, no. 1 (May 2003), http://www.austlii.edu.au/au/journals/PLPR/2003/17.html (accessed 1 June 2011).

17 Canadian Standards Association, Privacy Code (1996), "Principles in Summary," http://www.csa.ca/cm/ca/en/privacy-code/publications/view-privacy-code/article/principles-in-summary (accessed 10 February 2011).

18 Office of the Information and Privacy Commissioner, letter to Donna Hill regarding request for review P1583, 30 November 2010 (personal communication from Donna Hill).

19 In 2010, Alberta became the first jurisdiction in Canada to pass legislation that makes it mandatory to report a breach of privacy if there is significant risk of harm to the person whose information has been exposed. This is particularly noteworthy because Alberta journalists had been complaining that the provincial government had been exhibiting an increasing propensity to deny access to information requests.

20 Ruth Gavison, "Privacy and the Limits of Law," *Yale Law Journal* 89, no. 3 (1980): 465.

21 *R. v. Dersch*, [1993] 3 S.C.R. 768, Justice Claire L'Heureux-Dubé quoted at 785.

22 See Bobbie Johnson, "Privacy No Longer a Social Norm, Says Facebook Founder," guardian.co.uk, 11 January 2010, http://www.guardian.co.uk/technology/2010/jan/11/facebook-privacy (accessed 8 June 2010).

23 European Union, *Directive 95/46/EC*. Article 25 of the directive stipulates:

> 1 The Member States shall provide that the transfer to a third country of personal data which are undergoing processing or are intended for processing after transfer may take place only if, without prejudice to compliance with the national provisions adopted pursuant to the other provisions of this Directive, the third country in question ensures an adequate level of protection.
>
> 2 The adequacy of the level of protection afforded by a third country shall be assessed in the light of all the circumstances surrounding a data transfer operation or service of data transfer operations; particular consideration shall be given to the nature of the data, the purpose and duration of the proposed processing operation or operations, the country of origin and country of final destination. The rules of law, both general and sectoral, in force in the third country in question and the professional rules and security measures which are complied with in that country.

24 See Lorna Stefanick, "Outsourcing and Transborder Data Flows: The Challenge of Protecting Personal Information Under the Shadow of the USA Patriot Act," *International Review of Administrative Sciences* 73, no. 4 (December 2007): 531–48. The law prohibiting entry into the US of HIV-positive persons was rescinded in 2009.

25 Carol Tator and Frances Henry, with Charles Smith and Maureen Brown, *Racial Profiling in Canada: Challenging the Myth of "A Few Bad Apples,"* 56.

26 For details of the case, see Canada, Commission of Inquiry into the Actions of Canadian Officials in Relation to Maher Arar, *Report of the Events Relating to Maher Arar*.

27 Keith D. Smith, *Liberalism, Surveillance, and Resistance: Indigenous Communities in Western Canada, 1877–1927*, 52.

28 Ibid., 17.

29 Ibid., 112.

30 See the "Privacy Statement" and the downloadable PDF titled "Acknowledgement Statement" at City of Edmonton, Job Opportunities, http://www.edmonton.ca/city_government/jobs/job-opportunities-old.aspx (accessed 24 June 2010). As of June 2011, these materials could still be accessed, but as the "-old" in the URL indicates, the Job Opportunities page has been updated. The newer version (http://www.edmonton.ca/city_government/jobs/job-opportunities.aspx) omits the Privacy Statement, and the downloadable PDF ("Acknowledgment Form") has also been revised. The relevant statement now reads: "The City of Edmonton's online recruitment system is hosted by 'Taleo,' a U.S. company with locations in the United States, Canada, and Europe. . . . Taleo stores the information you provide to the City's online recruitment system on its server in Amsterdam, The Netherlands. The information will be protected with appropriate security safeguards, but may be subject to foreign law." It thus appears that Taleo now stores City of Edmonton data in Amsterdam rather than in the US.

31 Kenexa, "Why Assessments?" http://www.kenexa.com/assessments (accessed 8 June 2010).

32 David H. Flaherty, "Visions of Privacy: Past, Present, and Future," in *Visions of Privacy: Policy Choices for a Digital Age,* ed. Colin J. Bennett and Rebecca Grant, 21.

33 Canada, House of Commons Standing Committee on Human Rights and the Status of Persons with Disabilities, *Privacy: Where Do We Draw the Line?* Appendix I, "Privacy Rights and New Technologies: Consultation Package" 1.

CH_3
Freedom of Information (FOI)

1 Robert Cribb, "Dirty Dining," *Toronto Star*, http://caj.ca/wp-con tent/uploads/2010/mediamag/summer2001/caraward.html (accessed 10 February 2011). The first article in the series (which won the Canadian Association of Journalists' Best of the Best Award, Computer Assisted Reporting Category, in the summer of 2001) appeared on 19 February 2000.

2 British Columbia, Office of the Information and Privacy Commissioner for British Columbia, *2009–2010 Annual Report*, July 2010, 29–30, http://www.oipc.bc.ca/publications/annual_reports/OIPC_AR_2009_10.pdf (accessed 10 February 2011).

3 Canada, Commission of Inquiry into the Sponsorship Program and Advertising Activities, *Who Is Responsible? Phase 1 of the Report of the Commission of Inquiry into the Sponsorship Program and Advertising Activities (Gomery Commission).*

4 James Savage, "Member-State Budgetary Transparency in the Economic and Monetary Union," in *Transparency: The Key to Better Governance?* ed. Christopher Hood and David Heald, 148.

5 Jeffrey Owens, "Promoting Transparency and Co-operation in Financial Markets," *World Finance*, 13 May 2008, http://www.world finance.com/news/tax//article147.html (accessed 10 February 2011).

6 See David Banisar, "The Right to Information in the Age of Information," in *Human Rights in the Global Information Society,* ed. Rikke Frank Jørgensen, 77.

7 United Nations, "Universal Declaration of Human Rights," Article 19 http://www.un.org/en/documents/udhr/index.shtml (accessed 1 June 2011).

8 "Case of McGinley and Egan v. the United Kingdom," *International Journal of Human Rights* 2, no. 4 (1998): 135–37.

9 Open Society Justice Initiative, *Transparency and Silence: A Survey of Access to Information Laws and Practices in Fourteen Countries*, 74.

10 Banisar, "The Right to Information in the Age of Information," in *Human Rights in the Global Information Society*, ed. Jørgensen, 75.

11 "Nine Journalists Murdered, Four Disappeared in Mexico in 2010," *Borderland Beat: Reporting on the Mexican Cartel Drug War*, 3 January 2011, http://www.borderlandbeat.com/2011/01/nine-journalists-murdered-4-disappeared.html (accessed 11 February 2011).

12 "Guadalupe Mexico: Ericka Gandara, Last Police Officer, Missing," *The Huffington Post*, 28 December 2010, http://www.huffington post.com/2010/12/28/guadalupe-mexico-ericka-g_n_802091. html (accessed 3 January 2011).

13 *Marcel Claude Reyes and Others v. Chile* was the first ruling of the Inter-America's Court of Human Rights on access to information. It concerned the ability of the Terram Foundation, a Chilean environmental non-governmental organization, to access information from the Chilean Foreign Investment Committee concerning the environmental record of a US-based logging company that was planning a massive logging project on the Condor River.

14 Banisar, "The Right to Information in the Age of Information," in *Human Rights in the Global Information Society*, ed. Jørgensen, 80–81.

15 Dumisani Nyalunga, "The State of Access to Information in South Africa," IOLS-Research, University of KwaZulu-Natal, *Commentary*, July 2008 (accessed 16 December 2008 from http://iolsresearch.ukzn.ac.za/wonder16213.aspx, although the document is not currently available online). South Africa's most recent FOI legislation was enacted in 2001, Zimbabwe's and Angola's in 2002, and Uganda's in 2005.

16 Amartya Sen, quoted in Open Democracy Advice Centre, "About Us: Background to ODAC," http://www.opendemocracy.org.za/about/background/ (accessed 22 December 2008).

17 Open Society Justice Initiative, *Transparency and Silence*, 15–20.

18 Patrick Birkinshaw, "Transparency as a Human Right," in *Transparency*, ed. Hood and Heald, 49.

19 Ibid., 50.

20 Federal systems are those whose constitutions divide power between national and provincial or state governments. A unitary system has only a national government, which delegates power to sub-national levels. Examples of federal systems are Canada, the United States, and Australia. Examples of unitary systems are Britain, France, and New Zealand.

21 Declining trust in government is a global phenomenon. For a discussion of the situation in Canada, see Neil Nevitte, *The Decline of Deference: Canadian Value Change in Cross-National Perspective*, 54–59.

22 See Alasdair Roberts, "Dashed Expectations: Governmental Adaptation to Transparency Rules," in *Transparency*, ed. Hood and Heald, 107–26.

23 Open Society Justice Initiative, *Transparency and Silence*, 11–14.

24 See Alasdair Roberts, "Two Challenges in the Administration of the Access to Information Act," in *Research Studies Volume 2: The Public Service and Transparency*, ed. Commission of Inquiry into the Sponsorship Program and Advertising Activities, 115–62.

25 Roberts, "Dashed Expectations," in *Transparency*, ed. Hood and Heald, 110.

26 Ibid., 115.

27 "RCMP Probe Searches for Truth Behind Withheld Tory Flight Logs," *Calgary Herald*, 26 January 2009, http://www.canada.com/calgaryherald/news/story.html?id=dc9275a1-1cf2-4fbf-b332-112d42b3291d (accessed 10 February 2011).

28 Roberts, "Dashed Expectations," in *Transparency*, ed. Hood and Heald, 116.

29 For the book that popularized the notion of governments as "steering" rather than "rowing" the ship of state, see David Osborne and Ted Gaebler, *Reinventing Government: How the Entrepreneurial Spirit Is Transforming the Public Sector*.

30 See Andrew McDonald, "What Hope for Freedom of Information in the UK?" in *Transparency*, ed. Hood and Heald, 135.

31 Richard Mulgan, "Contracting Out and Accountability," 110.

32 See Alasdair Roberts, "Less Government, More Secrecy: Reinvention and the Weakening of Freedom of Information Law," *Public Administration Review* 6, no. 4 (July–August 2000): 308–20; and Lorna Stefanick, "Alberta's Ombudsman: Following Responsibility in an Era of Outsourcing," in *Provincial and Territorial Ombudsman Offices in Canada*, ed. Stewart Hyson, 25–52.

CH_ 4

Sharing Medical Information: Antidote or Bitter Pill?

1 Alan F. Westin and Vivian van Gelder, *Building Privacy by Design in Health Data Systems* (August 2005), 52, http://www.amia.org/files/ehrrept9-6-05_westin.pdf (accessed 2 May 2010).

2 *McInerney v. MacDonald* (1992), 93 D.L.R. (4th) 415 at 422 (S.C.C.).

3 M.A. Rodwin, *Medicine, Money and Morals: Physicians' Conflicts of Interest*, 268.

4 *R. v. O'Connor*, [1995] 4 S.C.R. 411, and *R. v. Mills*, [1999] 3 S.C.R. 668.

5 See World Medical Association, *Revised Declaration of Lisbon on the Rights of the Patient* (1981, with revisions in 1995 and 2005); World Health Organization, *A Declaration on the Promotion of Patient's Rights in Europe* (1994); and Council of Europe, Committee of Ministers, *Recommendation No. R (97) 5 of the Committee of Ministers to Member States on the Protection of Medical Data* (1997). All three documents are available online.

6 Westin and Gelder, *Building Privacy by Design*, 52.

7 For a detailed discussion of racial profiling, see Carol Tator and Frances Henry, with Charles Smith and Maureen Brown, *Racial Profiling in Canada: Challenging the Myth of "A Few Bad Apples."*

8 Canadian Human Rights Commission, "Canadian Human Rights Commission Policy on Alcohol and Drug Testing" (June 2002), 1–2, http://www.chrc-ccdp.ca/pdf/poldrgalceng.pdf (accessed 9 June 2010).

9 Manitoba, *Manitoba Ombudsman's Report into Garden Valley School Division's Proposed Policy "Drug Testing for Student Athletes,"* 16 September 2003, http://www.ombudsman.mb.ca/pdf/Final%20GVSD%20Consolidated%20Report.pdf (accessed 18 March 2010).

10 Jennifer D. Poudrier, "'Racial' Categories and Health Risks: Epidemiological Surveillance Among Canadian First Nations," in Surveillance as Social Sorting: Privacy, Risk, and Automated Discrimination, ed. David Lyon, 112.

11 See Jaakko Kaprio, "Science, Medicine and the Future: Genetic Epidemiology," British Medical Journal 320, no. 7244 (2000): 1257–59.

12 Michael Yudell, "A Short History of the Race Concept," Council for Responsible Genetics, GeneWatch 22, nos. 3–4 (July/August 2009), http://www.councilforresponsiblegenetics.org/genewatch/Gene WatchPage.aspx?pageId=198 (accessed 12 July 2011).

13 See Alberta's Sexual Sterilization Act, S.A. 1928, c.37, and Jana Grekul et al., "Sterilizing the 'Feeble-minded': Eugenics in Alberta, Canada, 1929–1972," Journal of Historical Sociology 17 (2004): 358–85. The Sterilization of Leilani Muir, a 1996 National Film Board documentary, is based on one Alberta woman's experience.

14 Robert Proctor, Racial Hygiene: Medicine Under the Nazis, 69.

15 See Burkart Holzner and Leslie Holzner, Transparency in Global Change: The Vanguard of the Open Society, 241–81.

16 Mary E. Schloendorff, Appellant v. The Society of the New York Hospital, Respondent, Court of Appeals of New York, 211 N.Y. 125; 105 N.E. 92 (decided 14 April 1914).

17 Henry K. Beecher, "Ethics and Clinical Research," The New England Journal of Medicine 274, no. 24 (1966): 1354–60.

18 Holzner and Holzner, Transparency in Global Change, 261.

19 Stephen B. Thomas and Sandra Crouse Quinn, "The Tuskegee Syphilis Study, 1932–1972: Implications for HIV Education and AIDS Education Programs in the Black Community," American Journal of Public Health 81, no. 11 (November 1991): 1498.

20 One need only use the Google search engine to find discussions of the racial inferiority of such groups as the Roma in Europe, illegal Mexican immigrants in the US, and Aboriginals in Canada. While the ideas promoted on such sites could be dismissed as coming from the lunatic fringe, they do underscore the problem of how easily scientific evidence can be distorted when it is viewed through the lens of racist assumptions.

CH_5
Surveillance in the Digital Age

1 Jeremy Bentham, *The Panopticon Writings,* ed. Miran Bozovic, Letter VI.

2 See Thomas Mathiesen, "The Viewer Society: Michel Foucault's 'Panopticon' Revisited."

3 David Murakami Wood, ed., *A Report on the Surveillance Society* (September 2006), 1, http://www.ico.gov.uk/upload/documents/library/data_protection/practical_application/surveillance_society_full_report_2006.pdf (accessed 3 June 2010).

4 Ibid., 4.

5 For these and other research findings, see Martin Gill and Angela Spriggs, *Assessing the Impact of CCTV,* 3–6. (A PDF of the report is available online; it can be located by a title search.)

6 Ibid., 3.

7 Philip Brey, "Ethical Aspects of Face Recognition Systems in Public Places," *Journal of Information, Communication and Ethics in Society* 2, no. 2 (2004): 97–109.

8 For a more complete discussion of how privatization affects accountability, see Lorna Stefanick, "Alberta's Ombudsman: Following Accountability in the Era of Outsourcing," in *Provincial and Territorial Ombudsman Offices in Alberta,* ed. Stewart Hyson, 27–52.

9   Nigel Waters, "Street Surveillance and Privacy," *Privacy Law and Policy Reporter* 32 (1996), www.austlii.edu.au/au/journals/PLPR/1996/32.html (accessed 16 December 2009).

10 Carol Tator and Frances Henry, with Charles Smith and Maureen Brown, *Racial Profiling in Canada: Challenging the Myth of "A Few Bad Apples,"* 56.

11 "Internet Game That Awards Points for People Spotting Real Crimes on CCTV Is Branded 'Snooper's Paradise,'" *Daily Mail Online,* 5 October 2009, http://www.dailymail.co.uk/news/article-1218225/Internet-game-awards-points-people-spotting-crimes-CCTV-cameras-branded-snoopers-paradise.html (accessed 2 May 2010), and Internet Eyes Blogspot, http://internet-eyes-news.blogspot.com/ (accessed 2 May 2010).

12 "ICO Puts Private Profit over Personal Privacy as Internet Eyes Game Launches," NO CCTV and Privacy International, press release, 1 October 2010, http://www.no-cctv.org.uk/press/press_release_14.pdf (accessed 4 February 2011).

13 Google Maps, "Behind the Scenes," http://maps.google.ca/help/maps/streetview/behind-the-scenes.html (accessed 9 February 2011).

14 StreetViewFun, http://www.streetviewfun.com/ (accessed 29 May 2010).

15 "Google May Drop Street View in EU If Photo Storage Time Is Cut," *Bloomberg Businessweek,* 2 March 2010, http://www.businessweek.com/news/2010-03-03/google-may-drop-street-view-in-eu-if-photo-storage-time-is-cut.html (accessed 2 May 2010).

16 Sid Maher, "Stephen Conroy Accuses Google of Biggest Privacy Breach in Western World," *The Australian,* 26 May 2010, http://www.theaustralian.com.au/business/media/conroy-accuses-

google-of-biggest-privacy-breach-in-western-world/story-e6frg
996-1225871306422 (accessed 26 May 2010).

17 "Google Streetview Faces Privacy Roadblocks in Japan, Greece,"
CBC NEWS, 13 May 2009, http://www.cbc.ca/world/story/2009/
05/13/google-street-view-japan-greece.html (accessed 29 May
2010).

18 "Privacy Watchdog to Sue Google Streetview," CBC News/Associ-
ated Press, 13 November 2009, http://www.cbc.ca/technology/
story/2009/11/13/tech-google-street-view-switzerland.html
(accessed 29 May 2010).

19 Letter from John M. Simpson, of Consumer Watchdog, to James
McPherson, executive director of the National Association of
Attorneys General, 26 May 2010, http://insidegoogle.com/wp-
content/uploads/2010/05/LTRNatAGS052610.pdf (accessed 26
May 2010). See also "Consumer Watchdog Urges State Attorneys General to Probe Google's WiSpy Snooping," Consumer
Watchdog, press release, 26 May 2010, http://insidegoogle.
com/2010/05/consumer-watchdog-urges-state-attorneys-
general-to-probe-googles-wispy-snooping/ (accessed 26 May
2010).

20 Organisation for Economic Co-operation and Development,
*Radio-Frequency Identification (RFID): Drivers, Challenges and Public
Policy Considerations*, 7.

21 Matt Ward, Rob van Kranenburg, and Gaynor Backhouse, *RFID:
Frequency, Standards, Adoption and Innovation*, 9.

22 Gal Eschet, "FIPs and PETs for RFID: Protecting Privacy in the
Web of Radio Frequency Identification," *Jurimetrics* 45, no. 301
(2005): 307–8.

23 Australian Law Reform Commission, *For Your Information: Australian Privacy Law and Practice*, vol. 1, sec. 9.39, p. 399, http://www.

austlii.edu.au/au/other/alrc/publications/reports/108/ (accessed 10 April 2010).

24 EPCglobal, "Guidelines on EPC for Consumer Products," http://www.epcglobalus.org/AboutUs/ConsumerAwareness/Consumer ProductGuidelines/tabid/197/Default.aspx (accessed 2 May 2010).

25 Philip J. Boyle and Kevin D. Haggerty, *Privacy Games: The Vancouver Olympics, Privacy and Surveillance,* http://www.sscqueens.org/sites/default/files/Privacy%20Games.pdf (accessed 3 June 2010).

26 Canada, Public Safety Canada, "2010 Olympic and Paralympic Winter Games: Security Budget: Allocation of Funds," http://www.publicsafety.gc.ca/media/nr/2009/nr20090219-1-eng.aspx (accessed 8 February 2011).

27 Canada, Office of the Parliamentary Budget Officer, "Assessment of Planned Security Costs for the 2010 G8 and G20 Summits," 23 June 2010, 4, http://www2.parl.gc.ca/sites/pbo-dpb/documents/SummitSecurity.pdf (accessed 7 February 2011).

28 Boyle and Haggerty, *Privacy Games,* 4.

29 Michael A. Gips, "Face-off over Facial Recognition," *Security Management* 45, no. 5 (2001): 12–14.

30 For an excellent example of the power of surveillance technologies when combined with social networking technology, see Port Moody photographer Ronnie Miranda's 2011 Stanley Cup project that aims to break the world record for the most people tagged in one online photo. Viewers can zoom in on a face in the crowd and tag the Facebook page so that the picture will appear on Facebook. See http://www.gigapixel.com/image/gigapan-canucks-g7.html.

31 "FactCheck: How Many CCTV Cameras?" Channel 4 News, 18 June 2008, http://www.channel4.com/news/articles/society/

factcheck+how+many+cctv+cameras/2291167 (accessed 5 July 2010).

32 "CCTV Boom Failing to Cut Crime," BBC News, 6 May 2008, http://news.bbc.co.uk/2/hi/uk_news/7384843.stm (accessed 1 May 2010).

33 Teneros, "Teneros Social Sentry™ Offers Breakthrough in Corporate Protection," http://www.teneros.com/socialsentry (accessed 2 May 2010); and Brian Sommer, "Big Brother Is Indeed Watching You: The Spy Side of Social Networking," ZDNET Business News Network, 6 April 2010, http://blogs.zdnet.com/sommer/?p=824 (accessed 2 May 2010).

34 Roger Clarke, "Introduction to Dataveillance and Information Privacy, and Definitions of Terms" (1997, with revisions in 1999, 2005, and 2006), http://www.anu.edu.au/people/Roger. Clarke/DV/Intro.html#DV (accessed 2 May 2010; the URL has since changed to http://www.rogerclarke.com/DV/Intro. html).

35 In 2009, the Electronic Privacy Information Center (EPIC) filed a FOI request with the US Department of Homeland Security (DHS) for records relating to the airport body scanner program. When the DHS failed to comply, EPIC sued, and the DHS released records revealing that, contrary to what authorities had said, the scanning machines were capable of storing and transmitting images. EPIC subsequently requested the release of some two thousand images of travellers' naked bodies that the DHS has in its possession, again resorting to a lawsuit to force compliance. As of June 2011, this case is still before the courts. See Electronic Privacy Information Center, "EPIC v. Department of Homeland Security — Body Scanners," http://epic.org/privacy/airtravel/backscatter/epic_v_dhs.html (accessed 9 February 2011).

36 "Employee Discounts and Employer Surveillance of Biometrics?" Sociological Images, 30 January 2010, http://thesocietypages. org/socimages/2010/01/30/employee-discounts-and-employer-surveillance-of-bio-metrics/ (accessed 4 June 2010).

37 See, for example, Herman Finer, "Administrative Responsibility in Democratic Government," *Public Administration Review* 1 (1941): 335–50; and Carl J. Friedrich, "Public Policy and the Nature of Administrative Responsibility" (1940), in *Public Policy*, ed. Carl Friedrich and Edward S. Mason, 3–24.

38 Noam Cohen and Brian Stelter, "Iraq Video Brings Notice to a Web Site," *New York Times*, 6 April 2010, http://www.nytimes. com/2010/04/07/world/07wikileaks.html (accessed 2 May 2010). The debate over whether Julian Assange is a hero or a villain was amplified in December 2010, when Sweden sought his extradition from Britain to face sexual assault charges. Defenders of Assange say the accusations are politically motivated.

39 WikiLeaks, "Collateral Murder," 5 April 2010, http://www.col lateralmurder.com/ (accessed 2 May 2010).

40 Richard Ackland, "Leaks Pour Forth from the Wiki Well of Information," *Sydney Morning Herald*, 9 April 2010, http://www. smh.com.au/opinion/politics/leaks-pour-forth-from-the-wiki-well-of-information-20100408-ruxn.html (accessed 7 February 2011); and Dan Froomkin, "WikiLeaks Video Exposes 2007 'Collateral Murder' in Iraq," *The Huffington Post*, 5 April 2010, http:// www.huffingtonpost.com/2010/04/05/wikileaks-exposes-video-0_n_525569.html (accessed 7 February 2011).

41 "US Says Wikileaks Could 'Threaten Global Security,'" BBC Mobile News: US and Canada, 26 July 2010, http://www.bbc.co. uk/news/world-us-canada-10758578 (accessed 8 February 2011).

CH_6
Social Networking: The Case of Facebook

1 Ronald Deibert and Rafal Rohozinski, "Introduction," in *Access Controlled: The Shaping of Power, Rights, and Rule in Cyberspace*, ed. Ronald J. Deibert, John G. Palfrey, Rafal Rohozinski, and Jonathan Zittrain, 3–4.

2 Danah M. Boyd and Nicole B. Ellison, "Social Network Sites: Definition, History, and Scholarship," *Journal of Computer-Mediated Communication* 13, no. 1, article 11 (2007).

3 Ibid. The question of who started Facebook is hotly contested. Various individuals, including Mark Zuckerberg, have laid claim to the original idea, with the predictable lawsuits ensuing. See, for example, John Markoff, "Who Founded Facebook? A New Claim Emerges," *New York Times*, 29 August 2007, http://www.nytimes.com/2007/09/01/technology/01facebook.html, and Nicholas Carlson, "At Last — the Full Story of How Facebook Was Founded," *Business Insider*, 5 March 1010, http://www.businessinsider.com/how-facebook-was-founded-2010-3 (both accessed 25 July 2011).

4 Mary Madden, "Reputation Management and Social Media: How People Monitor Their Identity and Search for Others Online," PewInternet: Pew Internet and American Life Project, 26 May 2010, http://www.pewinternet.org/~/media//Files/Reports/2010/PIP_Reputation_Management.pdf (accessed 30 May 2010).

5 Manuel Castells, Mireia Fernández-Ardèvol, Jack Linchuan Qiu, and Araba Sey, *Mobile Communication and Society: A Global Perspective*, 209.

6 Howard Rheingold, *Smart Mobs: The Next Social Revolution* (Cambridge: MIT Press, 2002). YouTube offers hundreds of examples of flash mob videos.

7 Virág Molnár, "Reframing Public Space Through Digital Mobilization: Flash Mobs and the Futility (?) of Contemporary Urban Youth Culture" (2010), http://isites.harvard.edu/fs/docs/icb.topic497840.files/Molnar_Reframing-Public-Space.pdf (accessed 21 May 2010).

8 Helen Murphy, "Colombians Stage 'Million Voices' March Against FARC," *Bloomberg*, 4 Februrary 2008, http://www.bloomberg.com/apps/news?pid=20601086&sid=aFXKi88tH.VE&refer=latin_america (accessed 21 May 2010).

9 A tweet is a text message or email of 140 characters maximum that is sent through the social networking service Twitter. Tweets are displayed on the author's profile page and delivered to the people who follow the author.

10 "'Support the Monks' via Facebook," *Toronto Star*, 30 September 2007, http://www.thestar.com/News/article/261973 (accessed 14 January 2011).

11 "In Memory of Neda Agha Soltan, 1982–2009," http://www.youtube.com/watch?v=DjGFlTDlHE4 (accessed 21 May 2010).

12 Jon Leyne, "How Iran's Political Battle Is Fought in Cyberspace," BBC News, 11 February 2010, http://news.bbc.co.uk/2/hi/middle_east/8505645.stm (accessed 21 May 2010).

13 See Rateb Joudeh, "Egypt: 'Social Network Revolt' with New Twists," *Rianovosti*, 15 February 2011, http://en.rian.ru/analysis/20110201/162405989.html (accessed 14 January 2011); and "The Face of Egypt's Social Networking Revolution: Wael Ghonim's Twitter and Facebook Activity Helped Spark the Egyptian Revolution, Causing Mubarak to Step Down as President," CBS Evening News, 12 February 2011, http://www.cbsnews.com/sections/eveningnews/main3420.shtml (accessed 14 January 2011).

14 Aaron Smith, "The Internet's Role in Campaign 2008," Pew Internet and American Life Project, 15 April 2009, http://pewresearch.org/pubs/1192/internet-politics-campaign-2008 (accessed 21 May 2010).

15 Harvey Jones and José Hiram Soltren "Facebook: Threats to Privacy" (December 2005), http://groups.csail.mit.edu/mac/classes/6.805/student-papers/fall05-papers/facebook.pdf (accessed 23 May 2010).

16 Ibid., 13. See also Joshua Fogel and Elham Nehmad, "Internet Social Network Communities: Risk Taking, Trust and Privacy Concerns," *Computers in Human Behavior* 25 (2009): 153–60; and Mariea Grubbs Hoy and George Milne, "Gender Differences in Privacy-related Measures for Young Adult Facebook Users," *Journal of Interactive Advertising* 10, no. 2 (Spring 2010): 28–45.

17 "Facebook Is a Feminist Issue," *Geek Feminism Blog: Women, Feminism, and Geek Culture,* 8 May 2010, http://geekfeminism.org/2010/05/08/facebook-is-a-feminist-issue/ (accessed 23 May 2010).

18 "Facebook, Privacy and Social Utility," *Larvatus Prodeo,* 16 May 2010, http://larvatusprodeo.net/2010/05/16/facebook-privacy-and-social-utility/ (accessed 23 May 2010).

19 Andrew Moran, "Facebook Founder Accused of Calling First Few Users 'Dumb,'" *Digital Journal,* 14 May 2010, http://www.digitaljournal.com/article/292032 (accessed 23 May 2010).

20 Zynga, "Fact Sheet," http://www.zynga.com/about/facts.php (accessed 23 May 2010).

21 Ginny Mies, "The Risks of Social Networking Games: They May Seem Benign, but Such Games Leave Players Vulnerable to Unwanted Recurring Charges and Security Threats," *PC World,* March 2010, 24 (accessed 22 May 2010).

22 Alex Li, "Connecting to Everything You Care About," The Facebook Blog, 19 April 2010, http://blog.facebook.com/blog.php?post=382978412130 (accessed 23 May 2010).

23 Facebook, "Facebook's Privacy Policy," http://www.facebook.com/policy.php (accessed 23 May 2010). The statement was revised again on 22 December 2010 to read:

> Information set to "everyone" is publicly available information, just like your name, profile picture, and connections. Such information may, for example, be accessed by everyone on the Internet (including people not logged into Facebook), be indexed by third party search engines, and be imported, exported, distributed, and redistributed by us and others without privacy limitations. Such information may also be associated with you, including your name and profile picture, even outside of Facebook, such as on public search engines and when you visit other sites on the internet. The default setting for certain types of information you post on Facebook is set to "everyone."

Although the wording is more detailed and complex, the substance of the policy remains unchanged.

24 Kurt Opsahl, "Facebook's Eroding Privacy Policy: A Timeline," Electronic Frontier Foundation, Deeplinks Blog, 28 April 2010, http://www.eff.org/deeplinks/2010/04/facebook-timeline/ (accessed 21 May 2010).

25 Senator Charles E. Schumer, "Schumer: Decision by Facebook to Share Users' Private Information with Third-party Websites Raises Major Privacy Concerns," press release, 25 April 2010, http://www.schumer.senate.gov/record.cfm?id=324175&

(accessed 23 May 2010). Interestingly, Schumer's statement is now available on Facebook — but, in the headline as it appears there, Facebook leaves out the word "Major" in front of "Privacy Concerns." See http://www.facebook.com/notes/chuck-schumer/ schumer-decision-by-facebook-to-share-users-private-infor mation-with-third-party/128806310575 (accessed 3 June 2011).

26 Canada, Office of the Privacy Commissioner, Elizabeth Denham, Assistant Privacy Commissioner of Canada, "Report of Findings into the Complaint Filed by the Canadian Internet Policy and Public Interest Clinic (CIPPIC) Against Facebook Inc. Under the *Personal Information Protection and Electronic Documents Act*," 16 July 2009, http://www.priv.gc.ca/cf-dc/2009/2009_008_0716_e.pdf (accessed 23 May 2010).

27 Canada, Office of the Privacy Commissioner, "Facebook Agrees to Address Privacy Commissioners Concerns," press release, 27 August 2009, http://www.priv.gc.ca/media/nr-c/2009/nr-c _090827_e.cfm (accessed 23 May 2010).

28 Richard Esguerra, "A Handy Facebook-to-English Translator," Electronic Frontier Foundation, Deeplinks Blog, 28 April 2010, https://www.eff.org/deeplinks/2010/04/handy-facebook-english- translator#connections (accessed 23 May 2010).

29 Both quoted in Sarah Schmidt, "Facebook Privacy Fight Heating Up: Experts Predict Federal Court Showdown by September," *Calgary Herald* (Canwest news service), 22 May 2010, http://www2. canada.com/calgaryherald/news/story.html?id=01b546c9-a715- 42da-9e3a-f8fac840fa58&p=2 (accessed 4 June 2011).

30 Sharon Gaudin, "More than Half of Facebook Users May Quit the Site, Poll Finds," *Computerworld,* 21 May 2010, http://www. computerworld.com/s/article/9177091/More_than_half_of_ Facebook_users_may_quit_site_poll_finds (accessed 23 May 2010).

31 See Matt Hartley, "FP Tech Desk: Quit Facebook Day Is May 31," *Financial Post*, 17 May 2010, http://business.financialpost. com/2010/05/17/fp-tech-desk-quit-facebook-day-is-may-31/ (accessed 23 May 2010). It is not very surprising that users had to go looking for information about how to delete accounts: it turns out that signing up is far easier than signing off. What Facebook calls "deletion" is set up as deactivation, which simply suspends the user's account, perhaps on the assumption that the user will eventually come to his or her senses and wish to reactivate the account. Actual deletion of an account is much more complex, and even then it is not immediate.

32 Castells, Fernández-Ardèvol, Qiu, and Sey, *Mobile Communication and Society*, 185.

33 James Grimmelmann, "Saving Facebook," *Iowa Law Review* 94 (2009): 1137–1206, http://works.bepress.com/james_grimmel mann/20/ (accessed 4 June 2011).

SELECTED BIBLIOGRAPHY

Ackland, Richard. "Leaks Pour Forth from the Wiki Well of Information." *Sydney Morning Herald*, 9 April 2010. http://www.smh.com.au/opinion/politics/leaks-pour-forth-from-the-wiki-well-of-information-20100408-ruxn.html.

Allen, Anita L. *Uneasy Access: Privacy for Women in a Free Society*. Totowa, NJ: Rowman and Littlefield, 1988.

Asia-Pacific Economic Cooperation. *APEC Privacy Framework*. Singapore: APEC Secretariat, 2005. http://www.apec.org/Groups/Committee-on-Trade-and-Investment/~/media/Files/Groups/ECSG/05_ecsg_privacyframewk.ashx.

Australia. Australian Law Reform Commission. *For Your Information: Australian Privacy Law and Practice*. ALRC Report no. 108. August 2008. http://www.austlii.edu.au/au/other/alrc/publications/reports/108/.

Banisar, David. "The Right to Information in the Age of Information." In *Human Rights in the Global Information Society*, edited by Rikke Frank Jørgensen, 73–90. Cambridge, MA: MIT Press, 2006.

BBC News. "CCTV Boom Failing to Cut Crime." http://news.bbc.co.uk/2/hi/uk_news/7384843.stm.

Beecher, Henry K. "Ethics and Clinical Research." *The New England Journal of Medicine* 274, no. 24 (1966): 1354–60.

Bentham, Jeremy. *The Panopticon Writings*. Edited by Miran Bozovic. London: Verso, 1995.

Boyd, Danah M., and Nicole B. Ellison. "Social Network Sites: Definition, History, and Scholarship." *Journal of Computer-*

Mediated Communication 13, no. 1, article 11 (2007). http://jcmc.
indiana.edu/vol13/issue1/boyd.ellison.html.

Boyle, Philip J., and Kevin D. Haggerty. *Privacy Games: The Vancouver Olympics, Privacy and Surveillance*. A Report to the Office of the Privacy Commissioner of Canada Under the Contributions Program. March 2009. http://www.sscqueens.org/sites/default /files/Privacy%20Games.pdf.

Brey, Philip. "Ethical Aspects of Face Recognition Systems in Public Places." *Journal of Information, Communication and Ethics in Society* 2, no. 2 (2004): 97–109.

Brown, B. *CCTV in Town Centres: Three Case Studies*. Home Office Police Research Group. Crime Prevention and Detection Series no. 73. London: HMSO, 1995.

Canada. Commission of Inquiry into the Actions of Canadian Officials in Relation to Maher Arar. *Report of the Events Relating to Maher Arar*. Ottawa: Canadian Government Publishing, 2006.

Canada. Commission of Inquiry into the Sponsorship Program and Advertising Activities. *Who Is Responsible? Phase 1 of the Report of the Commission of Inquiry into the Sponsorship Program and Advertising Activities (Gomery Commission)*. Ottawa: Canadian Government Publishing, 2005.

Canada. Department of Communications and Department of Justice. Task Force on Privacy and Computers. *Privacy and Computers: A Report of a Task Force Established Jointly by Dept. of Communications/Dept. of Justice*. Ottawa: Information Canada, 1972.

Canada. House of Commons Standing Committee on Human Rights and the Status of Persons with Disabilities. *Privacy: Where Do We Draw the Line?* Third Report, Second Session of the Thirty-fifth Parliament. Ottawa, April 1997. http:// www.priv.gc.ca/information/02_06_03d_e.pdf.

Canada. Office of the Parliamentary Budget Officer. "Assessment of Planned Security Costs for the 2010 G8 and G20 Summits."

23 June 2010. http://www2.parl.gc.ca/sites/pbo-dpb/documents/
SummitSecurity.pdf.

Canada. Office of the Privacy Commissioner. "Facebook Agrees
to Address Privacy Commissioners Concerns." Press release,
27 August 2009. http://www.priv.gc.ca/media/nr-c/2009/
nr-c_090827_e.cfm.

———. Elizabeth Denham, Assistant Privacy Commissioner of
Canada, "Report of Findings into the Complaint Filed by the
Canadian Internet Policy and Public Interest Clinic (CIPPIC)
Against Facebook Inc. Under the *Personal Information Protection
and Electronic Documents Act*." 16 July 2009. http://www.priv.
gc.ca/cf-dc/2009/2009_008_0716_e.pdf.

Canadian Human Rights Commission. "Canadian Human Rights
Commission Policy on Alcohol and Drug Testing." June 2002.
http://www.chrc-ccdp.ca/pdf/poldrgalceng.pdf.

Castells, Manuel, Mireia Fernández-Ardèvol, Jack Linchuan Qiu,
and Araba Sey. *Mobile Communication and Society: A Global
Perspective*. Cambridge, MA: MIT Press, 2007.

CBS Evening News. "The Face of Egypt's Social Networking Revolution: Wael Ghonim's Twitter and Facebook Activity Helped
Spark the Egyptian Revolution, Causing Mubarak to Step
Down as President." 12 February 2011. http://www.cbsnews.
com/sections/eveningnews/main3420.shtml.

Clarke, Roger. "Introduction to Dataveillance and Information
Privacy, and Definitions of Terms." 1997, with revisions in 1999,
2005, and 2006. http://www.rogerclarke.com/DV/Intro.html.

Council of Europe. Committee of Ministers. *Recommendation No.
R (97) 5 of the Committee of Ministers to Member States on the
Protection of Medical Data* (1997). https://wcd.coe.int/wcd/com.
instranet.InstraServlet?command=com.instranet.CmdBlobG
et&InstranetImage=564487&SecMode=1&DocId=560582&Us
age=2.

Cowen, Zelman. *The Private Man: The Boyer Lectures, 1969*. Sydney:
Australian Broadcasting Commission, 1969.

Deibert, Ronald J., John G. Palfrey, Rafal Rohozinski, and Jonathan Zittrain, eds. *Access Controlled: The Shaping of Power, Rights, and Rule in Cyberspace.* Cambridge, MA: MIT Press, 2010.

Deismann, W. *CCTV: Literature Review and Bibliography.* Research and Evaluation Detection Series no. 73. Ottawa: Royal Canadian Mounted Police, 2003.

Electronic Privacy Information Center. "EPIC v. Department of Homeland Security — Body Scanners." http://epic.org/privacy /airtravel/backscatter/epic_v_dhs.html.

Electronic Privacy Information Centre and Privacy International. *Privacy and Human Rights 2002: An International Survey of Privacy Laws and Developments.* www.privacyinternational.org/survey /phr2002/phr2002-part1.pdf.

Eschet, Gal. "FIPs and PETs for RFID: Protecting Privacy in the Web of Radio Frequency Identification." *Jurimetrics* 45, no. 301 (2005): 307–8.

Esguerra, Richard. "A Handy Facebook-to-English Translator." Electronic Frontier Foundation, Deeplinks Blog, 28 April 2010. https://www.eff.org/deeplinks/2010/04/handy-facebook-english-translator#connections.

Etzioni, Amitai. *The Limits of Privacy.* New York: Basic Books, 1999.

European Union. *Directive 95/46/EC of the European Parliament and of the Council of 24 October 1995 on the Protection of Individuals with Regard to the Processing of Personal Data and on the Free Movement of Such Data.* Official Journal L 281, 23 November 1995, 31–50. http://eur-lex.europa.eu/LexUriServ/LexUriServ. do?uri=CELEX:31995L0046:en:html.

Facebook. "Facebook's Privacy Policy." http://www.facebook.com/ policy.php.

"Facebook Is a Feminist Issue." *Geek Feminism Blog: Women, Feminism, and Geek Culture,* 8 May 2010. Accessed 23 May 2010 from http://geekfeminism.org/2010/05/08/facebook-is-a-feminist-issue/.

"Facebook, Privacy and Social Utility." *Larvatus Prodeo,* 16 May

2010. Accessed 23 May 2010 from http://larvatusprodeo.
net/2010/05/16/facebook-privacy-and-social-utility/.

Finer, Herman. "Administrative Responsibility in Democratic
Government." *Public Administration Review* 1 (1941): 335–50.

Flaherty, David H. "Visions of Privacy: Past, Present, and Future."
In *Visions of Privacy: Policy Choices for a Digital Age,* edited by
Colin J. Bennett and Rebecca Grant, 19–38. Toronto: Univer-
sity of Toronto Press, 1999.

Florini, Ann. "The End of Secrecy." In *Power and Conflict in the Age
of Transparency,* edited by Bernard I. Finel and Kristin M. Lord,
13–28. New York: Palgrave Macmillan, 2000.

Fogel, Joshua, and Elham Nehmad. "Internet Social Network
Communities: Risk Taking, Trust and Privacy Concerns."
Computers in Human Behavior 25 (2009): 153–60.

Foucault, Michel. *Discipline and Punish: The Birth of the Prison.* Trans-
lated by Alan Sheridan. New York: Random House, 1977.

Friedrich, Carl J. "Public Policy and the Nature of Administrative
Responsibility." In *Public Policy,* ed. Carl Friedrich and Edward
S. Mason, 3–24. Cambridge, MA: Harvard University Press,
1940.

Gavison, Ruth. "Privacy and the Limits of Law." *Yale Law Journal*
89, no. 3 (1980): 421–71.

Gill, Martin, ed. *CCTV.* Leicester: Perpetuity Press, 2003.

Gill, Martin, and Angela Spriggs. *Assessing the Impact of CCTV.*
Home Office Research Study no. 292. London: HMSO, 2005.
(Available as a PDF online.)

Grekul, Jana, et al. "Sterilizing the 'Feeble-minded': Eugenics in
Alberta, Canada, 1929–1972." *Journal of Historical Sociology* 17
(2004): 358–85.

Grimmelmann, James. "Saving Facebook." *Iowa Law Review* 94
(2009): 1137–1206. http://works.bepress.com/james_grimmel
mann/20/.

Grubbs Hoy, Mariea, and George Milne. "Gender Differences in
Privacy-related Measures for Young Adult Facebook Users."
Journal of Interactive Advertising 10, no. 2 (Spring 2010): 28–45.

Hartley, Matt. "FP Tech Desk: Quit Facebook Day Is May 31." *Financial Post*, 17 May 2010. http://business.financialpost. com/2010/05/17/fp-tech-desk-quit-facebook-day-is-may-31/.

Holzner, Burkart, and Leslie Holzner. *Transparency in Global Change: The Vanguard of the Open Society.* Pittsburgh: University of Pittsburgh Press, 2006.

Hood, Christopher, and David Heald, eds. *Transparency: The Key to Better Governance?* Proceedings of the British Academy no. 135. Oxford: Oxford University Press, 2006.

Johnson, Bobbie. "Privacy No Longer a Social Norm, Says Facebook Founder." *Guardian.co.uk*, 11 January 2010. http://www. guardian.co.uk/technology/2010/jan/11/facebook-privacy.

Johnson, Tim. "The Wild Web." *University Affairs*, 6 October 2008. http://www.universityaffairs.ca/the-wild-web.aspx.

Jones, Harvey, and José Hiram Soltren. "Facebook: Threats to Privacy." Unpublished paper, December 2005. http://groups. csail.mit.edu/mac/classes/6.805/student-papers/fall05-papers/facebook.pdf.

Joudeh, Rateb. "Egypt: 'Social Network Revolt' with New Twists." *Rianovosti*, 15 February 2011. http://en.rian.ru/analysis/20110201/162405989.html.

Kaprio, Jaakko. "Science, Medicine and the Future: Genetic Epidemiology." *British Medical Journal* 320, no. 7244 (2000): 1257–59.

Kirby, Michael. "Privacy Protection, a New Beginning: OECD Principles Twenty Years On." *Privacy Law and Policy Reporter* 6, no. 3 (1999). http://www.austlii.edu.au/au/journals/PLPR/1999/41.html.

Li, Alex. "Connecting to Everything You Care About." *The Facebook Blog*, 19 April 2010. http://blog.facebook.com/blog.php?post=382978412130.

Lord, Kristin M. *The Perils and Promise of Global Transparency: Why the Information Revolution May Not Lead to Security, Democracy, or Peace.* Albany, NY: SUNY Press, 2006.

Lyon, David, ed. *Surveillance as Social Sorting: Privacy, Risk, and Automated Discrimination*. London and New York: Routledge, 2003.

MacKinnon, Catharine. *Toward a Feminist Theory of the State*. Cambridge, MA: Harvard University Press, 1989.

Madden, Mary. "Reputation Management and Social Media: How People Monitor Their Identity and Search for Others Online." Pew Internet and American Life Project, 26 May 2010. http://www.pewinternet.org/~/media//Files/Reports/2010/PIP_Reputation_Management.pdf.

Maher, Sid. "Stephen Conroy Accuses Google of Biggest Privacy Breach in Western World." *The Australian*. http://www.theaustralian.com.au/business/media/conroy-accuses-google-of-biggest-privacy-breach-in-western-world/story-e6frg996-1225871306422.

Manitoba. *Manitoba Ombudsman's Report into Garden Valley School Division's Proposed Policy "Drug Testing for Student Athletes."* 16 September 2003. http://www.ombudsman.mb.ca/pdf/Final%20GVSD%20Consolidated%20Report.pdf.

Mathiesen, Thomas. "The Viewer Society: Michel Foucault's 'Panopticon' Revisited." *Theoretical Criminology* 1, no. 2 (1997): 215–34.

Meade, Ellen E., and D. Stasavage. *Publicity of Debate and the Incentive to Dissent: Evidence from the U.S. Federal Reserve*. London: Royal Institute for International Affairs, 2004.

Mies, Ginny. "The Risks of Social Networking Games: They May Seem Benign, but Such Games Leave Players Vulnerable to Unwanted Recurring Charges and Security Threats." *PC World* 28, March 2010.

Molnár, Virág. "Reframing Public Space Through Digital Mobilization: Flash Mobs and the Futility (?) of Contemporary Urban Youth Culture." Unpublished paper, 2010. http://isites.harvard.edu/fs/docs/icb.topic497840.files/Molnar_Reframing-Public-Space.pdf.

Moran, Andrew. "Facebook Founder Accused of Calling First Few Users 'Dumb.'" *Digital Journal,* 14 May 2010. Accessed 23 May 2010 from http://www.digitaljournal.com/article/292032.

Mulgan, Richard. "Contracting Out and Accountability." *Australian Journal of Administration* 56, no. 4 (December 1997): 106–16.

Murakami Wood, David, ed. *A Report on the Surveillance Society.* A report produced by the Surveillance Studies Network for the Information Commissioner of the United Kingdom. September 2006. http://www.ico.gov.uk/upload/documents/library/data_protection/practical_application/surveillance_society_full_report_2006.pdf.

Nevitte, Neil. "Citizens' Values, Information, and Democratic Life." Government of Canada, Access to Information Review Task Force, Report no. 2. March 2001. http://www.atirtf-geai.gc.ca/paper-citizen-e.html.

———. *The Decline of Deference: Canadian Value Change in Cross-National Perspective.* Peterborough, ON: Broadview Press, 1996.

Norris, Clive, Jade Moran, and Gary Armstrong, eds. *Surveillance, Closed Circuit Television and Social Control.* Aldershot, UK: Ashgate, 1998.

Nyalunga, Dumisani. "The State of Access to Information in South Africa." IOLS-Research, University of KwaZulu-Natal. *Commentary,* July 2008.

Open Society Justice Initiative. *Transparency and Silence: A Survey of Access to Information Laws and Practices in Fourteen Countries.* New York: Open Society Institute, 2006.

Opsahl, Kurt. "Facebook's Eroding Privacy Policy: A Timeline." Electronic Frontier Foundation, *Deeplinks Blog,* 28 April 2010. http://www.eff.org/deeplinks/2010/04/facebook-timeline/.

Organisation for Economic Co-operation and Development. *Implementation Plan for the OECD Guidelines for the Security of Information Systems and Networks: Towards a Culture of Security.* 2 July 2003. http://www.oecd.org/dataoecd/23/11/31670189.pdf.

————. *Guidelines on the Protection of Privacy and Transborder Flows of Personal Data.* 1980. http://www.oecd.org/document/18/0, 3746,en_2649_34255_1815186_1_1_1_1,00.html.

————. *Radio-Frequency Identification (RFID): Drivers, Challenges and Public Policy Considerations.* OECD Digital Economy Papers no. 110. OECD Publishing, 2006. http://dx.doi.org/10.1787/231551650432.

Orwell, George. *Nineteen Eighty-Four.* Harmondsworth, UK: Penquin, 1954.

Osborne, David, and Ted Gaebler. *Reinventing Government: How the Entrepreneurial Spirit Is Transforming the Public Sector.* Reading, MA: Addison-Wesley, 1992.

Owens, Jeffrey. "Promoting Transparency and Co-operation in Financial Markets." *World Finance*, 13 May 2008. http://www.worldfinance.com/news/tax//article147.html.

Painter, Kate, and Nick Tilley. *Surveillance of Public Space: CCTV, Street Lighting and Crime Prevention.* Monsey, NY: Criminal Justice Press, 1999

Poudrier, Jennifer D. "'Racial' Categories and Health Risks: Epidemiological Surveillance Among Canadian First Nations." In *Surveillance as Social Sorting: Privacy, Risk, and Automated Discrimination*, edited by David Lyon, 111–34. London and New York: Routledge, 2003.

Proctor, Robert. *Racial Hygiene: Medicine Under the Nazis.* Cambridge, MA: Harvard University Press, 1988.

Rheingold, Howard. *Smart Mobs: The Next Social Revolution.* Cambridge, MA: MIT Press, 2002.

Roberts, Alasdair. *Blacked Out: Government Secrecy in the Information Age.* Cambridge: Cambridge University Press, 2006.

————. "Less Government, More Secrecy: Reinvention and the Weakening of Freedom of Information Law." *Public Administration Review* 6, no. 4 (July–August 2000): 308–20.

————. "Two Challenges in the Administration of the Access to Information Act." In *Research Studies Volume 2: The Public Service*

and Transparency, ed. Commission of Inquiry into the Sponsorship Program and Advertising Activities, 115–62. Ottawa:
Public Works and Government Services Canada, 2006.

Rodwin, M.A. *Medicine, Money and Morals: Physicians' Conflicts of
Interest*. Oxford: Oxford University Press, 1993.

Schumer, Senator Charles E. "Schumer: Decision by Facebook to
Share Users' Private Information with Third-party Websites
Raises Major Privacy Concerns." Press release, 25 April 2010.
http://www.schumer.senate.gov/record.cfm?id=324175&.

Smith, Aaron. "The Internet's Role in Campaign 2008." Pew
Internet and American Life Project, 15 April 2009. http://
pewresearch.org/pubs/1192/internet-politics-campaign-2008.

Smith, Keith D. *Liberalism, Surveillance, and Resistance: Indigenous
Communities in Western Canada, 1877–1927*. Edmonton: Athabasca University Press, 2009.

Sommer, Brian. "Big Brother Is Indeed Watching You: The Spy
Side of Social Networking." ZDNET Business News Network,
6 April 2010. http://blogs.zdnet.com/sommer/?p=824.

Stefanick, Lorna. "Alberta's Ombudsman: Following Account-
ability in the Era of Outsourcing." In *Provincial and Territorial
Ombudsman Offices in Alberta*, edited by Stewart Hyson, 27–52.
Toronto: University of Toronto Press, 2009.

———. "Outsourcing and Transborder Data Flows: The Challenge
of Protecting Personal Information Under the Shadow of the
USA Patriot Act." *International Review of Administrative Sciences*
73, no. 4 (December 2007): 531–48.

Tan, Johanna G. "A Comparative Study of the APEC Privacy
Framework — a New Voice in the Data Protection Dialogue?"
Asian Journal of Comparative Law 3, no. 1 (2008).

Tator, Carol, and Frances Henry, with Charles Smith and Maureen
Brown. *Racial Profiling in Canada: Challenging the Myth of "A Few
Bad Apples."* Toronto: University of Toronto Press, 2006.

Taylor, Fredrick Winslow. *The Principles of Scientific Management*.
New York: W.W. Norton, 1967.

Thomas, Stephen B., and Sandra Crouse Quinn. "The Tuskegee Syphilis Study, 1932–1972: Implications for HIV Education and AIDS Education Programs in the Black Community." *American Journal of Public Health* 81, no. 11 (November 1991): 1498–1504.

Tilley, Nick. *Understanding Car Parks, Crime and CCTV: Evaluation Lessons from Safer Cities.* Crime Prevention Unit Series no. 42. London: HMSO, 1993.

Ward, Matt, Rob van Kranenburg, and Gaynor Backhouse. *RFID: Frequency, Standards, Adoption and Innovation.* Joint Information Systems Committee (JISC) Technology and Standards Watch, May 2006.

Warren, Samuel, and Louis D. Brandeis. "The Right to Privacy." *Harvard Law Review* 4, no. 5 (1890): 193–220.

Waters, Nigel. "Street Surveillance and Privacy." *Privacy Law and Policy Reporter* 32 (1996). www.austlii.edu.au/au/journals/PLPR/1996/32.html.

Welsh, Brandon C., and David P. Farrington. *Crime Prevention Effects of Closed Circuit Television: A Systematic Review.* Home Office Research Study no. 252. London: HMSO, 2002.

Westin, Alan F. *Privacy and Freedom.* New York: Atheneum, 1967.

Westin, Alan F., and Vivian van Gelder. *Building Privacy by Design in Health Data Systems.* A report by the Program on Health Information Technology, Health Records and Privacy, Center for Social and Legal Research, Hackensack, NJ. August 2005. http://www.amia.org/files/ehrrept9-6-05_westin.pdf.

WikiLeaks. "Collateral Murder." 5 April 2010. http://www.collateral murder.com/.

Wilson, Dean, and Adam Sutton. *Open-Street CCTV in Australia: A Comparative Study of Establishment and Operation.* A Report to the Criminology Research Council, April 2003. Canberra: Criminology Research Council, 2003. http://www.criminology researchcouncil.gov.au/reports/200102-26.pdf.

INDEX

cellphones, 51, 153, 162, 164–65

censorship, 19, 75, 76, 139, 158

Chile: access legislation in, 75, 213n13

Clarke, Roger, 151

"Collateral Murder" (US military video), 154

commodification: and Facebook, 175–76; of information, 207n13; of personality, 174

confidentiality, 34–35, 97–98, 103–4, 106–8

Conroy, Stephen, 139

consent. See informed consent

"coverage creep," 42

Cowen, Zelman, 34

crime: and access to information legislation, 70, 74–75; and data matching, 49–50; and sharing of medical information, 99; and transparency, 9–10; and video surveillance, 131–33, 135, 136–37, 148

D

data banks: and employment application forms, 54–55; and data flow concerns, 46–51; and data matching, 48–51, 109–11; and data mining, 42–43, 49; maintained by governments, 43–44; privacy concerns

about, 11, 16–17; and privacy directives, 38; and secondary uses of medical information, 111–21; and sharing of medical information, 98–99, 109–11 databases. See data banks

"dataveillance," 151

Department of Indian Affairs (Canada): and surveillance, 53

digital divide, 18–19

drug testing, 56, 109–10

E

e-commerce, 44–45

educational institutions, 58–59, 83, 131, 206n10

electronic health record (EHR), 98–103

Electronic Privacy Information Center (EPIC), 222n35

email, 86

employee assessments, 55–56

employment applications: and privacy, 54–55, 59

EPCglobal Incorporated, 144

eugenics, 117–18

European Union (EU): privacy directives of, 39–40, 45–46, 210n23

F

Facebook: deleting accounts on, 182–84, 228–29n31; description of, 158–61;

and Internet surveillance,
139, 165; and mega-events,
146; social network sites
and, 164–66; and out-
sourcing of services, 89–91;
and WikiLeaks, 153–54
group rights. *See* individual
versus group rights

H
Heald, David, 8
human rights, 73–74, 76

I
ICTs (information and communication technologies),
187–88, 192, 194
individual versus group rights:
and access/privacy debate,
3–4; in health research, 120–
21; and the Internet, 158;
in management of medical
information, 99; and public
interest, 67, 71; and ramifi-
cations of FOIP, 5–7
information: and digital
communications technol-
ogy, 1–2; filtering of, 20–22;
management of, 4, 7, 42–43
information and communication technologies (ICTs),
187–88, 192, 194
informed consent, 118–19
Internet: and access to infor-

mation legislation, 90;
commodification of, 174–76;
debate over control of, 19–
20, 158; and e-commerce,
44–45; history of, 2; privacy
concerns surrounding,
17–18; and video surveil-
lance, 136–41; and virtual
communities, 161, 162–66;
and WikiLeaks, 153–54, 156.
See also Facebook; Google
Internet Eyes game, 136–38
Iran: 2009 presidential elections
in, 164–65

J
Japan: and Google Street View,
140
Jones, James, 155

K
King, Rodney: beating of by LA
police, 153
knowledge: as power, 14–15, 18,
127

L
La Forest, Gérard, 37–38

M
MacKinnon, Catherine, 13–14
Mathiesen, Thomas, 127–28
*McGinley and Egan v. the United
Kingdom*, 72

190–91; concepts related to, 34–36; and concerns surrounding biometrics, 151–52; and concerns surrounding data flow, 46–51; and concerns surrounding Facebook, 166–72; cultural differences regarding, 140–41; and cultural norms, 30–32; definitions of, 29–30, 34, 36, 59–60; effect of security surveillance on, 152–54; effect of technology on, 33, 41, 42–45; and good governance, 17–18, 22, 92; in historical perspective, 33–34; as human right, 12, 37; and ideology, 32–33; international directives on, 38–41, 45–46; of medical health information, 100–103; promotion of as new industry, 46; and radio-frequency identification devices, 143–44; as recognized in Canadian law, 37–38; relationship of to transparency, 10, 12; relinquishment of control over, 51–52, 54; and divide between rich and poor, 52–53, 59, 135, 190; and video surveillance, 132,

133–36, 137–41; workplace invasions of, 54–58, 59. *See also* privacy protection
Privacy and Freedom (Westin), 38
Privacy International, 46, 137
privacy protection: and adoption, 106–8; and Facebook, 160–61, 166–67, 171, 173–74, 177–84, 227n23; and health research, 115–21; and information held by government, 65–66; and medical information, 103–6, 111–15, 118; and medical profiling, 109–11; in private sector, 24, 41–42, 94–95; and radio-frequency identification devices, 144–45; relationship of to freedom of information, 23–24; and "security function creep," 147–48
private sector: and access to information legislation, 24, 65, 94; and control of private information, 51, 189; and data flow, 46–47; and freedom of information, 21, 64–65, 70; and mega-events, 146; and privacy legislation, 24, 41–42, 94–95; as provider of security, 145; and radio-frequency identification

transparency, 9–10, 16; by
governments of civilians,
53–54; of Indigenous
peoples, 53; at mega-
events, 147–48; and radio-
frequency identification
devices, 142–45; theories
of, 126–28; types of, 125–26,
128–30; by video cameras,
130–41, 148–49; of women,
54; at the workplace, 55–57,
149–50, 151. *See also*
panopticon; synopticon
synopticon, 128, 130

T

Taylor, Frederick, 149
technology: and data flow
concerns, 46–51; and
dissent, 153–54; effect
of on communication,
187; effect of on privacy,
33, 41, 42–45; and
"function creep," 148, 149;
government attempts
to control, 157–58; and
information explosion,
1–2; and management of
information, 42–43; and
speed of information,
17–18. *See also* radio-
frequency identification
device; video cameras
terrorism, 49, 145, 146

transparency: balance with
privacy, 7, 60–61, 93,
94–95, 97–98, 191–95;
different forms of, 8–10;
of Facebook, 166–72; and
filtering of information,
20–22; and government
outsourcing, 89–91; in
medical records, 99–100,
101–3; as part of good
governance, 13–16, 22,
63–64; relationship with
privacy, 10, 12; and sur-
veillance of authority,
125–26, 153–55. *See also*
databases; freedom of
information; surveillance
Tuskegee syphilis study, 119–20
Twitter, 153, 164, 225n9

U

United Kingdom (UK): access
legislation in, 78; and
CCTVs, 133, 136–37, 140,
149; and Google Street
View, 140
United States: and access to
health information, 108;
access to information
legislation in, 72, 78–79;
data matching/mining
in, 49; and Facebook
privacy policy, 179–80;
government transparency

RECYCLED
Paper made from
recycled material
FSC
www.fsc.org   FSC® C103567

Marquis Book Printing Inc.

Québec, Canada
2011

Printed on Silva Enviro 100% post-consumer EcoLogo certified paper,
processed chlorine free and manufactured using biogas energy.